CodeIgniter 1.7 Professional Development

Become a CodeIgniter expert with professional tools, techniques, and extended libraries

Adam Griffiths

BIRMINGHAM - MUMBAI

CodeIgniter 1.7 Professional Development

First published: April 2010

Production Reference: 1190410

Published by Packt Publishing Ltd.
32 Lincoln Road
Olton
Birmingham, B27 6PA, UK.

ISBN 978-1-849510-90-5

`www.packtpub.com`

Cover Image by Filippo (`filosarti@tiscali.it`)

Credits

Author
Adam Griffiths

Reviewers
Jose Argudo
Saidur Rahman

Acquisition Editor
Dilip Venkatesh

Development Editor
Dilip Venkatesh

Technical Editor
Aaron Rosario

Indexer
Monica Ajmera Mehta

Editorial Team Leader
Akshara Aware

Project Team Leader
Lata Basantani

Project Coordinator
Joel Goveya

Proofreader
Dirk Manuel

Production Coordinator
Shantanu Zagade

Cover Work
Shantanu Zagade

About the Author

Adam Griffiths is a student and freelance CodeIgniter Developer based in the United Kingdom. He has five years of web development experience, the last two being largely influenced by CodeIgniter. He has worked on many websites, both large and small, from small blogs to large websites for multi-national corporate companies. He is well versed in development techniques and how to squeeze that little bit more from an application. He has also made a number of contributions to the CodeIgniter Community, most notably The Authentication Library, a very simple to use but full-featured Authentication Library for CodeIgniter.

When CodeIgniter and PHP aren't spiralling around his head, Adam enjoys practising card and mentalism tricks, mainly sleight of hand and card handling tricks. He has performed at local and formal functions for hundreds of people. He is also a guitar player and enjoys playing acoustically at pubs and small gigs. Moving back towards computing, he has a deep interest in Cryptography. He loves finding patterns in data and loves using pen and paper to decipher any cipher text he may find around the web. Find out more and read his blog at `http://www.adamgriffiths.co.uk`.

I would like to thank my parents for encouraging me to better myself. If it weren't for them I may not have written this book. I would also like to thank my friends for letting me bounce ideas off of them and develop these ideas. I've wanted to write a book for a while now, so a big thank you goes to Packt Publishing for giving me this opportunity; and to everybody involved in reviewing, editing, and managing the book as a whole.

To the readers—Thank you for purchasing this book. It means a great deal to me that you will be reading the content that I spent a lot of time on, and you will hopefully learn a lot from it.

About the Reviewers

Jose Argudo is a web developer from Valencia, Spain. After finishing his studies he started working for a web design company. Six years later, he decided to start working as a freelancer.

Now that some years have passed as a freelancer, he thinks it's the best decision he has ever taken—a decision that let him work with the tools he likes, such as Joomla!, Codeigniter, Cakephp, Jquery, and other well-known open source technologies.

His desire to learn and share his knowledge has led him to be a regular reviewer of books from Packt, such as Joomla! With Flash, Joomla! 1.5 SEO, Magento Theme Design or Symfony 1.3 web application development.

Recently he has even published his own book, Codeigniter 1.7, which you can also find at Packt's site. If you work with PHP, take a look at it!

If you want to know more about him, you can check out his site at `www.joseargudo.com`

To my girlfriend and to my brother, I wish them the best.

Saidur Rahman Bijon is an open source enthusiast from Bangladesh. He graduated in computer science in from BRAC university and has been developing web applications for over four years. In this time, he has developed ecommerce, web 2.0, social networking, and microblogging applications. He shares his knowledge and ideas at `http://saidur.wordpress.com`.

He started his career by developing a large scale application for the Bangladesh Navy. Since then, he has worked mainly for Japanese and USA based outsourcing companies, where he has built applications in CodeIgniter. Currently, he is working for a USA based company, Blueliner Bangla (`http://www.bluelinerny.com/`) as a senior software engineer.

> I'd like to thank Packt for giving me the opportunity to review this book.
>
> I enjoyed it thoroughly.
>
> I'm really thankful for my family, friends, and colleagues for their help and support.

I dedicate this book to my family.

Table of Contents

Preface

This book takes you beyond the CodeIgniter user guide and into more advanced subjects that you need to know if you plan to use CodeIgniter on a daily basis. The book will teach you how to build libraries in order to complete different tasks and functions. You will create mini-applications each of which teaches a specific technique and builds on top of the CodeIgniter base. By the time that you finish this book you will be able to create a CodeIgniter application of any size with confidence, ease, and speed.

What this book covers

Chapter 1, Getting Started with CodeIgniter—This chapter guides you from installing CodeIgniter to learning about its URL structure, the MVC design pattern, helpers, plugins, and extending and replacing libraries.

Chapter 2, Learning the Libraries—You are taken through a number of the core CodeIgniter libraries, being introduced to each library, what it does and how you go about using it. Some libraries work together, and if this is the case, then this chapter explains how they can be used together.

Chapter 3, Form Validation and Database Interaction—Form validation is a task that some users find difficult. This chapter focuses on teaching you the correct way to validate your forms, by using the Form Validation library. You will also cover the Database library and Database Forge, a way to easily manage database tables.

Chapter 4, User Authentication 1—The first User Authentication chapter focuses on building your own authentication system. We build a model that handles the registration and logging in of users. We also include a function to check whether a user is logged in or not.

Chapter 5, User Authentication 2—The second and final User Authentication chapter focuses solely on user log-in in through Twitter oAuth and Facebook Connect. For each example the CodeIgniter code is explained, as well as how both company's APIs work, and to some extent how each differs from the other.

Chapter 6, Application Security—This chapter discusses how CodeIgniter is secure by design, for example, disallowing certain characters in the URI strings. We also go over what you can do to make your CodeIgniter application more secure than a default installation.

Chapter 7, Building a Large-Scale Application—This chapter takes you through some of the techniques that you can use to make your CodeIgniter application scalable. You learn about identifying bottlenecks via benchmarking results, caching, using better PHP functions, optimizing SQL queries, and using memcache and multiple application instances.

Chapter 8, Web Services—This chapter builds an example web service by using the REST principle. This includes a simple client library that issues requests, and a server library that deals with requests and responds as appropriate.

Chapter 9, Extending CodeIgniter—This chapter covers everything you need to know about extending CodeIgniter's default functionality without hacking at the core files. This is very useful, especially when it is time to upgrade to the newest version of CodeIgniter.

Chapter 10, Developing and Releasing Code to the Community—In this chapter you will learn how to release code to the community, gain exposure for your released code, and how to properly maintain the code and give good support to those using your code.

Who this book is for

This book is written for advanced PHP developers with a good working knowledge of Object Oriented Programming techniques who are comfortable with developing applications and wish to use CodeIgniter to make their development easier, quicker and more fun. Basic knowledge of CodeIgniter will be helpful. This book will suit developers who fall into three categories:

- Professional Developers—Employees of a software house or other type of development company
- Freelance Developers—A sole developer working in the industry on their own
- Just for fun Developer—A person using PHP to build web applications is their spare time for fun

Conventions

In this book, you will find a number of styles of text that distinguish between different kinds of information. Here are some examples of these styles, and an explanation of their meaning.

Code words in text are shown as follows: "We can include other contexts through the use of the `include` directive."

A block of code is set as follows:

```
[default]
exten => s,1,Dial(Zap/1|30)
exten => s,2,Voicemail(u100)
exten => s,102,Voicemail(b100)
exten => i,1,Voicemail(s0)
```

When we wish to draw your attention to a particular part of a code block, the relevant lines or items are set in bold:

```
[default]
exten => s,1,Dial(Zap/1|30)
exten => s,2,Voicemail(u100)
exten => s,102,Voicemail(b100)
exten => i,1,Voicemail(s0)
```

Any command-line input or output is written as follows:

```
# cp /usr/src/asterisk-addons/configs/cdr_mysql.conf.sample
    /etc/asterisk/cdr_mysql.conf
```

New terms and **important words** are shown in bold. Words that you see on the screen, in menus or dialog boxes for example, appear in the text like this: "clicking on the **Next** button moves you to the next screen".

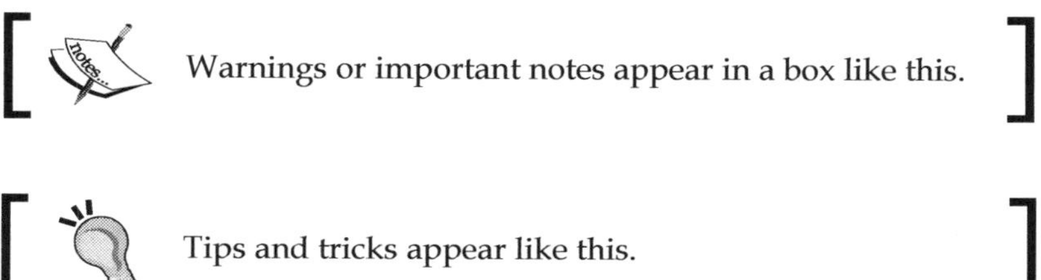

Warnings or important notes appear in a box like this.
Tips and tricks appear like this.

Reader feedback

Feedback from our readers is always welcome. Let us know what you think about this book—what you liked or may have disliked. Reader feedback is important for us to develop titles that you really get the most out of.

To send us general feedback, simply send an e-mail to feedback@packtpub.com, and mention the book title in the subject of your message.

If there is a book that you need and would like to see us publish, please send us a note via the **SUGGEST A TITLE** form on www.packtpub.com, or send an e-mail to suggest@packtpub.com.

If there is a topic that you have expertise in and you are interested in either writing or contributing to a book on, see our author guide on www.packtpub.com/authors.

Customer support

Now that you are the proud owner of a Packt book, we have a number of things to help you to get the most from your purchase.

Downloading the example code for the book

Visit http://www.packtpub.com/files/code/0905_Code.zip to directly download the example code.

The downloadable files contain instructions on how to use them.

Errata

Although we have taken every care to ensure the accuracy of our content, mistakes do happen. If you find a mistake in one of our books—maybe a mistake in the text or the code—we would be grateful if you would report this to us. By doing so, you can save other readers from frustration and help us to improve subsequent versions of this book. If you find any errata, please report them by visiting http://www.packtpub.com/support, selecting your book, clicking on the **let us know** link, and entering the details of your errata. Once your errata are verified, your submission will be accepted and the errata will be uploaded on our website, or added to any list of existing errata, under the Errata section of that title. Any existing errata can be viewed by selecting your title from http://www.packtpub.com/support.

Piracy

Piracy of copyright material on the Internet is an ongoing problem across all media. At Packt, we take the protection of our copyright and licenses very seriously. If you come across any illegal copies of our works, in any form, on the Internet, please provide us with the location address or website name immediately so that we can pursue a remedy.

Please contact us at `copyright@packtpub.com` with a link to the suspected pirated material.

We appreciate your help in protecting our authors, and our ability to bring you valuable content.

Questions

You can contact us at `questions@packtpub.com` if you are having a problem with any aspect of the book, and we will do our best to address it.

1
Getting Started with CodeIgniter

CodeIgniter is an open source web application framework for the PHP language. CodeIgniter has many features that make it stand out from the crowd. Unlike some other PHP frameworks you may have come across, the documentation is very thorough and complete—covering every aspect of the framework. CodeIgniter will also run in shared hosting environments as it has a very low footprint, yet it still has exceptional performance.

On the programming side, CodeIgniter is both PHP4 and PHP5 compatible, so it will run on the majority of web hosts out there. It also uses the **Model View Controller** (**MVC**) design pattern, which is a way to organize your application into three different parts: models—the database abstraction layer, views—the front end template files, and controllers—the business logic of your applications. In the core, CodeIgniter also makes extensive use of the Singleton design pattern. This is a way to load classes so that if they are called multiple times, the same instance of the class will be returned. This is highly useful for database connections, as you would only want one connection each time that the class is used.

CodeIgniter also has an implementation of the Active Record pattern. This makes it easy to write complex SQL queries and makes your application more readable. Active Record also allows you to easily swap and change database drivers. This allows you to write the queries in PHP and still use a MySQL backend, and also gives you the option to switch to an Oracle database -without having to rewrite the queries in your application.

CodeIgniter also comes with a number of highly useful libraries and other sets of functions that help you to build your applications. This leaves you to focus on the small part of your application that is unique, rather than the part that is used across all projects, such as database queries and parsing data.

In this chapter, we will:

- Install CodeIgniter
- Learn about the MVC Design Pattern
- Learn how to format your code according to the CodeIgniter PHP Style Guide
- Learn how CodeIgniter URLs work
- Learn about CodeIgniter-specific files

Upgrading from older versions of CodeIgniter

Users on older versions of CodeIgniter should upgrade to the latest version for a number of reasons.

Firstly, each new release comes with many bug fixes, and more importantly, security patches. This makes applications running on older versions of CodeIgniter more vulnerable to attack than the newer versions.

There are also more features. For example, a new Cart Library was introduced in CodeIgniter 1.7, allowing users to build a simple shopping cart application easily, using a native supported library rather than a third-party one.

To upgrade to CodeIgniter 1.7, follow the instructions given next and simply migrate your application folder over to the newer codebase.

Downloading and installing CodeIgniter

This book assumes prior knowledge of PHP—this should also stretch to a web server. CodeIgniter needs a web server to run on, just like any other PHP application. You can install CodeIgniter locally just for testing, or use it on your current web server; anywhere will suffice.

Getting the CodeIgniter files

The first step to getting started with CodeIgniter is to download the files from the website. The website is located at `www.codeigniter.com`. This website includes a backlog of all of the previous versions of CodeIgniter, as well as a **Subversion Repository** (**SVN**) for the latest version. In our case, we can simply download the latest version straight from the home page—currently 1.7.2— by clicking on the **Download CodeIgniter** button, as seen in the next screenshot.

When you have downloaded the ZIP file, unzip it using your favourite file archiving program. You will now have a folder named `CodeIgniter_1.7.2`. The folder should contain two files and two directories, as seen in the next screenshot.

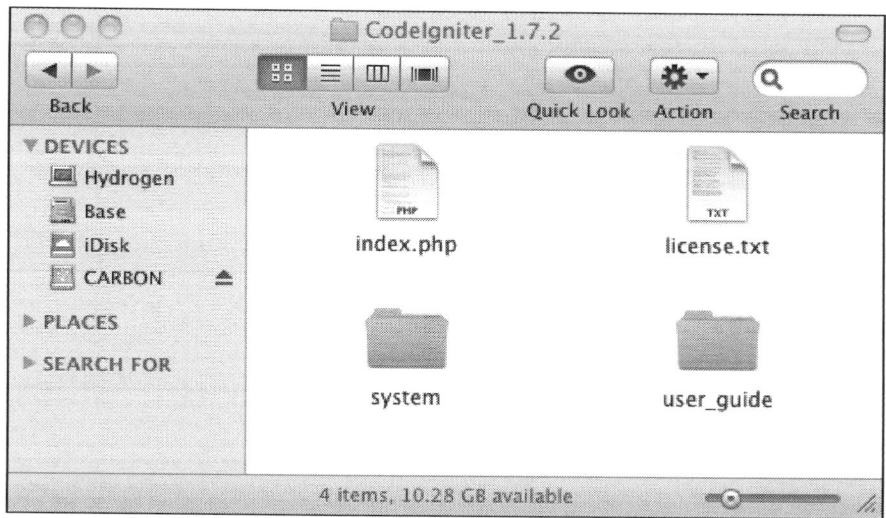

The `system` directory holds the core CodeIgniter files, libraries, and other CI specific stuff, such as the logs and cache directories. It also houses the `application` folder—this is the only folder you truly need to worry about, as this is the only place where you need to put your files. As you can guess, this is the folder where all your application-specific code goes, and includes the configuration files that you may need to edit.

Simply open this folder in your code editor of choice and we'll go ahead and install CodeIgniter in our final step. We need to edit the base URL—the URL at which you will you access your application—and to do this we need to open the file `/system/application/config/config.php`. The value that we need to change is the array item `$config['base_url']` which is currently set to `http://example.com/`—simply change this to your URL.

> The base URL value needs to have a trailing slash (a forward slash) at the end.

When that is done, navigate to your base URL and you should see the CodeIgniter welcome screen, as seen in the next screenshot.

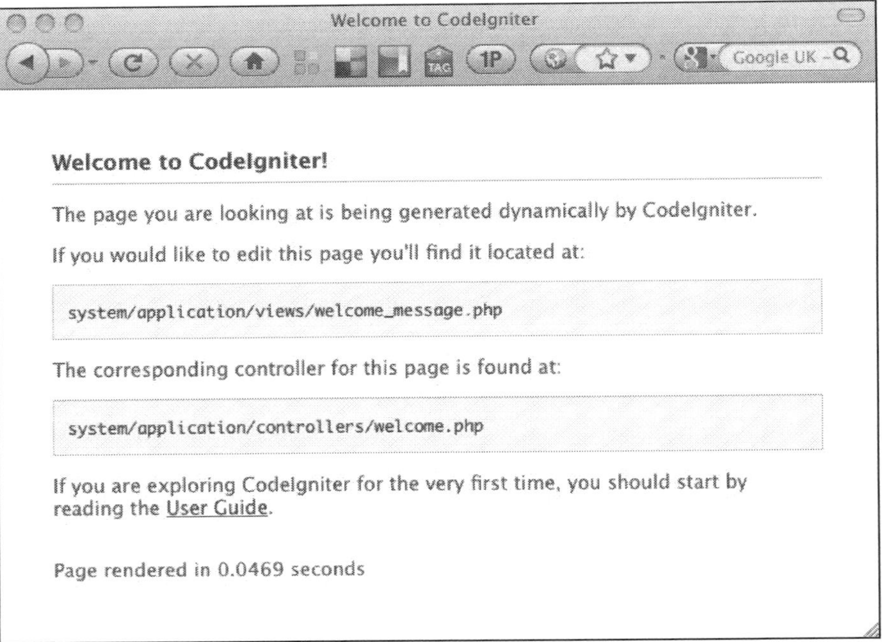

Introducing Model View Controller (MVC)

Although you have heard this term mentioned in this book already, you may not know what the term means. In short, **Model View Controller**—from now on, referred to as MVC—is a software development design pattern. MVC is an approach to separating your applications into three segments: **Models**, **Views**, and **Controllers**. MVC structures your application in this way in order to promote the reuse of program code.

The **Model** represents any type of data that your application may use. Some examples of data that your application might use would be: a database, RSS Feeds, API calls, and any other action that involves retrieving, returning, updating, and removing data.

Views are the information that is being presented on the screen to users through their web browsers. These are usually HTML files, sometimes containing PHP code that builds the template for the website. In CodeIgniter however, views can be page segments, partial templates, or any other type of page or template.

Finally, **Controllers** are the business logic of your application. They serve as an intermediary between Models and Views. The Controller will respond to HTTP requests and generate web pages.

However, CodeIgniter's approach to MVC is very loose. This means that Models are not required. This is for a number of reasons. Firstly, CodeIgniter's Database Library can be used in both Models and Controllers—meaning that the extra separation of Models can be bypassed. Secondly, the Model isn't tied to the database, as it is in other frameworks such as Ruby on Rails, so the Model isn't needed in this regard. Finally, if using a Model in your application will cause unnecessary complexity, then the Model can simply be ignored.

However, Models are extremely useful, even though they are optional. Models can be loaded from any Controller, so if you use a Model function in multiple controllers and you need to change the function, you only need to edit it in one place rather than in all of the controllers. Complex queries should really be put into a Model. A collection of related queries should also be put into a Model as they can be grouped together. This makes your applications simpler, and it allows you to use the functions in any Controller.

Controllers: The business logic

Controllers are the core of your application because they determine how HTTP requests should be handled. Let's dive right in and create a simple Hello World controller. Create a file called `helloworld.php` in `system/application/controllers/`.

```
<?php
  class Helloworld extends Controller
  {

    function HelloWorld()
    {
      parent::Controller();
    }

    function index()
    {
      echo("Hello, World!");
    }
  }
?>
```

Let's dissect this controller to get a better understanding of controllers.

Firstly, you can see that the controller is a class that extends the base **Controller** class. The next thing to note is that there is a function with the name `index`. This is the default function, and will be called when another function has not been called. To see this being run, simply navigate to the URL `http://yourwebsite.ext/index.php/helloworld/` and you should see the words **Hello, World!** on the screen.

All Controller class names should start with an uppercase letter, and the rest of the name should be lowercase. Controllers should always extend the base class so that you can use all of CodeIgniter's syntax and have access to all CI resources.

If you have a constructor in your Controller then you need to call upon the `Controller` constructor, as we have in the example HelloWorld Controller. You should call it as follows:

```
Parent::Controller();
```

Defining a default Controller

CodeIgniter has the ability to set a Controller as the default controller. This is the controller that is to be called when no other controller is passed to `index.php`. A default CodeIgniter install will set the default controller to `welcome_message.php`– this is the default CI welcome page, as shown earlier.

To set a different default controller, open the file `system/application/config/routes.php` and change `welcome` to the name of any other controller in your application.

```
$route['default_controller'] = "welcome";
```

Remapping function calls

You can remap function calls by using a function in your controller called `_remap()` — this will be called every time that the controller is called, even if a different function is used. This is useful for developers who wish to easily remap their function calls in order to provide a different **Uniform Resource Identifier** (**URI**) structure, or to remap functions instead of extending CodeIgniter's routing class.

The function string will be passed to the function. You would usually have a function that looks like this:

```
Function _remap($method)
{
  if($method == "method_name")
  {
    $this->$method();
  }
  else
  {
    $this->default_method();
  }
}
```

Models: Data abstraction layer

Now that you know what a Model is and what it's used for, we can take a look at how to construct a Model.

Models are stored in `system/application/models/`. The class of your model should have the first letter capitalized and the rest of the name lowercase, and also extend the base class of Model. The class should also have a constructor that calls upon the base class constructor, as seen in the next code example.

```
<?php
class Mymodel extends Model
{
  funcion Mymodel()
  {
    parent::Model();
  }
}
?>
```

The filename of this model should be an all-lowercase version of the name; the filename therefore will be `mymodel.php`.

Loading a Model

A model is loaded from Controller functions. Loading a model takes just one line of code.

```
$this->load->model('model_name');
```

In this instance, you should replace `model_name` with the name of your model. If your model is located in a sub-folder, you would load the model as follows:

```
$this->load->model('sub_folder/model_name');
```

Once loaded, you access your model functions by using the global object with the same name as your model name.

```
$this->model_name->function_name();
```

You can assign a new name for your Model object by passing it to the second parameter of the loading function.

```
$this->load->model('model_name', 'different_name');
```

Now you would call your model functions as follows:

```
$this->different_name->function_name();
```

Here's an example of a controller calling a model and serving a view.

```
<?php
class Shop extends Controller
{
  function Shop()
  {
    parent::Controller();
  }

  function index()
  {
    $this->load->model('products');
    $products = $this->products->build_list();
    $this->load->view('shop', $products);
  }
}
?>
```

Connecting to your database automatically

When a model is loaded, it does not connect to the database automatically unless you autoload the database class for your application. You can tell the model to connect to the database automatically by passing boolean `TRUE` as the third parameter.

```
$this->load->model('model_name', '', TRUE);
```

The model will now connect to the database using the setting defined in your `database.php` configuration file, which is located in `system/application/config/`.

You can pass an array of configuration details to the third parameter if you wish to use a database other than the one that's set up in your database configuration file.

```
$config['hostname'] = "localhost";
$config['username'] = "myusername";
$config['password'] = "mypassword";
$config['database'] = "mydatabase";
$config['dbdriver'] = "mysql";
$config['dbprefix'] = "";
$config['pconnect'] = FALSE;
$config['db_debug'] = TRUE;

$this->load->model('model_name', '', $config);
```

Views: Your template files

Views are your template files. They are what is output to the browser, and should be mostly HTML code, with some PHP code. Put simply, views are HTML files of your template; they can also be page segments, such as a header or footer. View files can also call other views, if you need such flexibility.

Views are located in the `system/application/views/` folder, and can be stored in subfolders inside this main `views` folder.

Loading a view

Loading a view is done in the same way as loading a model; it takes just one line of code.

```
$this->load->view('view_name');
```

Here, `view_name` would be the name of the view file that you wish to load. You can also pass an array of data to a view file by passing an array as the second parameter of the `load->view` function.

```
$data['title'] = "My Web Page";
$this->load->view('view_name', $data);
```

You would then be able to use the variable `$title` in your view file to echo out the page title.

Loading multiple views

You load multiple views in the same way as you load just one view. CodeIgniter intelligently handles multiple calls to `$this->load->view`, and will append these calls together. Here is an example:

```
function index()
{
  $data['title'] = "My Web Page";
  $this->load->view('header', $data);
  $this->load->view('navigation');
  $this->load->view('content');
  $this->load->view('footer');
}
```

Adding dynamic data

Adding data to a view file is a very simple process, which we have touched upon already. You pass data to a view file by using the second parameter of the `load->view` function. All view data must be passed as an array or an object. This is because CI runs this array or object through PHP's extract function, which simply takes an object or array key and creates a variable for it with the same name. Let's look at an example:

```
$data = array(
      'title' => "My Web Page",
      'heading' => "Welcome to my web page",
      'content' => "This is my first web page using Codeigniter!"
      );
$this->load->view('main', $data);
```

You will then be able to use this data in your view, as illustrated below:

```
<html>
<head>
  <title><?php echo $title; ?></title>
</head>
<body>
<h1><?php echo $heading; ?></h1>
<?php echo $content; ?>
</body>
</html>
```

Creating loops

Creating loops in view files has been a stumbling block for a few developers. By passing a multidimensional array to a view file, you can easily establish a loop in any of your view files. Let's take a look at an example.

```
<?php
  class Todo extends Controller
  {
    function index()
    {
      $data['todo_list'] = array("buy food", "clean up", "mow lawn");
      $this->load->view('todo', $data);
    }
  }
?>
```

This is a very simple Controller. Your view file for this would be as follows:

```
<html>
<head>
  <title><?php echo $title; ?></title>
</head>
<body>
<h1><?php echo $heading; ?></h1>
<?php echo $content;?>
<h2>My Todo List</h2>
<?php
foreach($todo_list as $item)
{
  echo $item;
}
?>
</body>
</html>
```

Returning views as data

You are also able to return view files as data; this can be useful if you wish to process this data in some way. Simply set the third parameter to boolean TRUE—and it will return the view data.

```
$this->load->view('welcome', NULL, TRUE);
```

CodeIgniter uses an output buffer to take all calls to the load view function, and processes them all at once, sending the whole page to the browser at the same time. So when you return views as data, you will be able to save the contents of the view inside a variable for whatever use you need.

Autoloading resources

CodeIgniter comes with built-in functionality that enables you to load libraries, plugins, helpers, models, and so on, on each request. This is useful for database intensive applications, as you can autoload the Database Library so that you won't need to load it yourself.

Simply open up the application/config/autoload.php file and put the name of the library or other type of file that you want to autoload into the appropriate array.

Formatting your code—PHP Style Guide

CodeIgniter does not force any specific coding style on you as a developer. However there is a PHP Style Guide that sets a number of rules that you can use when developing for CodeIgniter. These are mostly style rules to help your code fit in with the core code better, as the core development team follows these rules, as well as those of us who develop using the framework. I will not go over the entire style guide, but I will highlight the most noteworthy conventions.

PHP closing tag

The PHP closing tag ?> is optional to the PHP parser. If used, any whitespace after the PHP closing tag can result in PHP errors, warnings, or even blank pages. For this reason, all PHP files should omit the closing PHP tag, and instead use a comment block to display relevant details for the file location. This allows you to signify that a file is complete.

Incorrect

```
<?php
  class Helloworld extends Controller
  {
    function index()
    {
      echo("Hello, World!");
    }
  }
?>
```

Correct

```
<?php
  class Helloworld extends Controller
  {
    function index()
    {
      echo("Hello, World!");
    }
  }

/* End of file helloworld.php */
/* Location: system/application/controllers/ */
```

Class and method naming

As we have touched upon before, class names should always have their first letter in uppercase and the rest of the name in lowercase. Multiple words should be separated with an underscore and not use the CamelCase convention.

Incorrect

```
class myClass
class MYClass
```

Correct

```
class My_class
```

The class and constructor method should have identical names. Take this example:

```
class My_class
{
  function My_class()
  {

  }
}
```

Here is a set of examples of improper and proper method naming, taken directly from the PHP Style Guide of the CodeIgniter user guide.

Incorrect

```
function fileproperties() // not descriptive and needs underscore
                          // separator
function fileProperties() // not descriptive and uses CamelCase
function getfileproperties() // Better! But still missing underscore
                             // separator
function getFileProperties() // uses CamelCase
function get_the_file_properties_from_the_file() // wordy
```

Correct

```
function get_file_properties() // descriptive, underscore separator,
                               // and all lowercase letters
```

Variable names

The guidelines for variable names are very similar to those for class and method names. Variable names should only contain lowercase letters, should use underscore separators to separate words and not use CamelCasing, and should be named to indicate their contents.

Incorrect

```
$f = 'foo'; // single letter variable name, does not explicitly show
            //what it contains
$Text // contains uppercase letters
$someTextHere // uses camelCase and does not show it's contents
$userid // multiple words, needs an underscore to separate them
```

Correct

```
for ($i = 0; $i <= 10; $i++)
$text
$user_id
```

Commenting

CodeIgniter recommends that you comment your code as much as possible. This is for two reasons: it helps inexperienced programmers who may be working on the same project as you, or if you release your code; and it will help you months down the line to understand the code more quickly than if there were no comments. There isn't a particular required commenting style, but CodeIgniter recommends that you use DocBlock styling. This is recommended as it will be picked up by many **Integrated Development Environments** (IDE).

```
/**
* Class Name
*
* @package Package name
* @subpackage Subpackage Name
* @category category name
* @author Author Name
* @linkhttp://example.com
*/
```

When commenting your code, you should use singe line comments and leave a line between a large comment block and the code. I would personally recommend that comments mean something.

Poor

```
// a foreach loop

foreach($posts as $post)
{
  echo $post;
}
```

Good

```
// loop through the blog posts and echo each out

foreach($posts as $post)
{
  echo $post;
}
```

This is my personal recommendation, because silly comments such as the first won't help you a few months down the line, simply because you can already tell it's a `Foreach` loop.

Use of TRUE, FALSE, and NULL

When using the keywords TRUE, FALSE, and NULL in your applications, you should always write them in uppercase letters.

Incorrect

```
if($active == true)
$zero = null;
function test($test = false)
```

Correct

```
if($active == TRUE)
$zero = NULL;
function test($test = FALSE)
```

Short opening tags

You should always use full PHP opening tags and not short tags, just in case a server does not have `short_open_tag` enabled. CodeIgniter can rewrite short tags, although the PHP Style Guide states that full opening tags should be used.

Incorrect

```
<? echo $foo; ?>
<?=$foo?>
```

Correct

```
<?php echo $foo; ?>
```

One statement per line

You should always have one statement per line in CodeIgniter applications. This improves code readability, and will also makes things easier to find.

Incorrect

```
$foo = 'bar'; $bar = 'foo'; $baz = 'zip';
```

Correct

```
$foo = 'bar';
$bar = 'foo';
$baz = 'zip';
```

CodeIgniter URLs

CodeIgniter URLs use **Uniform Resource Identifiers (URI)**. In simple terms, CodeIgniter's URLs are simply segments. These segments are then split up and used to load a particular controller and method. Here is a typical CodeIgniter URL:

```
http://mywebsite.ext/index.php/controller/method/parameters
```

Everything after the `index.php` segment is used by CodeIgniter to determine what to load. The first segment is the name of the Controller. The second segment is used to determine which function to load—if this is blank then the index function will be used. The final segment will be used to pass any data to the function.

Removing the index.php file

You can remove the `index.php` part of the URL by adding a `.htaccess` file to the root of your CodeIgniter install. Here is an example file:

```
RewriteEngine on
RewriteCond $1 !^(index\.php|images|robots\.txt)
RewriteRule ^(.*)$ /index.php/$1 [L]
```

This will redirect anything to the `index.php` file except for `index.php`, the `images` folder, and `robots.txt`. You can add any other items to the list as you so wish, such as a folder for `.css` files or even JavaScript files.

Adding a URL Suffix

You can specify in your `system/application/config/config.php` file to add a suffix to your URLs. Take this example:

```
http://mywebxite.ext/products/books/
```

You can add a suffix so that the URL becomes:

```
http://mywebsite.ext/products/books.html
```

You don't have to use `.html`, I just used it as an example.

CodeIgniter specific files

CodeIgniter has a number of different file types that can be used in your applications to make your job easier. These are helpers, plugins, and libraries. They all differ in some way, with their own unique abilities.

Helpers

Helper files are a collection of functions in a particular group. For example, CodeIgniter has a URL helper, which lets you easily print your website URL or the current URL, build links, and a few other functions too. Helpers can be used within Models, Controllers, and View files.

Helpers are not written in an object oriented format in the way that Controllers and Models are, they are simply a collection of procedural functions.

Loading a helper

Loading a helper is just like loading anything else in CodeIgniter; it takes just one line of code.

```
$this->load->helper('form');
```

Loading multiple helpers

You can load multiple helpers by passing an array of values to the first parameter.

```
$this->load->helper( array('form', 'url', 'cookie') );
```

Using a helper

Because helper files are procedural files, you simply use the function in the same way as you call a standard PHP function, and not in the objective format as you would with models.

For example, to echo your site URL using the URL helper, you would use:

```
<?php echo base_url(); ?>
```

"Extending" Helpers

Even though helpers are procedural files, you can extend them in a literal sense. To do this, create a file in the `system/application/helpers/` folder, with the same name as a core CI helper with the prefix `MY_`. You can change this prefix, but we won't go into that right now.

Then you simply create a function inside this file with the same name as the function that you wish to replace, or add a new function.

For example, if you wanted to extend the `Form Helper`, you would create a file called `MY_form_helper.php` inside the `system/application/helpers/` folder, and create any functions that you wish to add.

Plugins

Plugins work in almost exactly the same way as Helpers. The main difference is that a plugin should be used to add a single function, instead of a collection of functions. Helpers are also considered to be part of the core framework, whereas plugins are intended to be created and shared by the community. Plugins are stored inside the `system/application/plugins/` folder.

Loading a plugin

Loading a plugin is almost the same as loading a helper. The only difference is the function used.

```
$this->load->plugin('name');
```

Where `name` is the name of the plugin you wish to load.

Loading multiple plugins

To load more than one plugin, simply pass an array to the load function.

```
$this->load->plugin( array('name1', 'name2', 'name3') );
```

Using a plugin

Once a plugin is loaded, you simply call it in the same way as you would call a standard PHP function.

Libraries

Libraries provide extra functionality that can be used across multiple projects. Libraries usually abstract functions for many different tasks. For example, the Database Library provides a way to create SQL functions in very simple, readable ways. It is advisable to keep Library calls out of your View files, and a helper should be used to perform the operation instead.

Creating your own libraries

You can easily create your own libraries. The first step in creating a library is to create a file inside the `system/application/libraries/` folder, with a relevant name; you should also take the naming conventions outlined in the style guide into account.

The next step is to create a class inside this file, with the same name as your PHP file—but without the `.php` extension. You do not need to extend any classes when creating your own library.

Using CodeIgniter resources within your library

When using CodeIgniter, you load helpers, libraries, and other resources by using the super object **$this->**. However, when creating your own library, you will not have access to this unless you explicitly add it in by using the following function:

```
$CI =& get_instance();
```

Once you do this inside a function, you would use **$CI** in place of **$this** when utilizing CodeIgniter resources.

Using your class

To load your library, you simply use the following function:

```
$this->load->library('name');
```

Where `name` is the name of the library you wish to load.

Extending core libraries

To extend a core CodeIgniter library, first create a file with the same name as the library you wish to extend, but add the `MY_` prefix. For example, to extend the `Session` class, create a file called `MY_Session.php` and place it inside the `system/application/libraries` folder. Once this is done, you simply extend the core library as follows:

```
<?php
  class MY_Session extends CI_Session
{
    function MY_Session()
    {
      parent::CI_Session();
    }
}
?>
```

Loading your extended library

You load your extended library in exactly the same way as you load the core library. In our example, we'd use the following line of code. Note that I do not include the `MY_` prefix.

```
$this->load->library('session');
```

Replacing core libraries

Replacing core libraries is similar to extending them. Instead of using the `MY_` prefix in your file name and class name, you drop the prefix for the filename and use the prefix `CI_` for the class name. This is because all CodeIgniter core libraries have the prefix `CI_`. Staying with the session class, we would replace it as follows:

```
<?php
  class CI_Session
  {

  }
?>
```

To load the library, you would do so as if you hadn't changed anything:

```
$this->load->library('session');
```

Summary

Well done. You've made it through *Chapter 1*. That's all you need to know to get started with CodeIgniter. In *Chapter 2, Learning the Libraries*, we'll go over some of the great libraries that CodeIgniter comes with, taking you to a higher level of knowledge.

2
Learning the Libraries

CodeIgniter comes with a set of class files that are used throughout many applications—these are known as "Libraries". In short, a library is a file that helps developers write better code, build better applications, and become more productive through the use of abstracted functions. A library creates a wrapper for your application's functions which, for example, enables you to swap database drivers without changing any code. In this chapter you will learn:

- How to benchmark your application
- How to send e-mails and create a contact form
- How to create a file uploader
- General application security points
- Pagination
- Using CodeIgniter sessions
- How to run unit tests

What is a library?

A CodeIgniter library is simply a class file that abstracts functionality into easy-to-use functions that take much of the strain off the developer. Take the Database Library as an example. It contains many functions that make the creation of complex SQL queries very easy; it also makes queries much more readable. The terms "class" and "library" are used interchangeably throughout this chapter.

Project-specific libraries are located in the `system/application/libraries/` folder and all of the CodeIgniter core libraries are located in the `system/libraries/` folder.

What do libraries do?

Libraries abstract out functionality for developers and make it easy to re-use code. CodeIgniter comes with many core libraries that provide ways to code your applications much faster than without libraries, removing much of the unnecessary code from your applications, and taking the strain off the developer.

There are many types of libraries included with CodeIgniter, and many more released by community members. In this chapter, we will cover the eight most important libraries.

Every library has a different set of collected functions, but all work to make coding applications much simpler than they would be if you were not using a framework.

Benchmarking Class

The Benchmarking Class is used to calculate the time between two points in your application. It's always ON, which means you do not need to load the library before using it. The timing between the two points that you specify in your application is very accurate because this library is loaded at the same time as CodeIgniter, and ended by the output class immediately before data is sent to the browser.

Benchmarking is important in any application that should expect a large number of users. If, at some point, you realize that your application is slowing down for users at any one point, you can run a benchmark to find out where the bottleneck is, and how to remedy it.

Setting a benchmark

Creating a Benchmark is a very simply process. Benchmarks can be added to Controllers, Views, and Models in three simple steps:

1. Mark the starting point.
2. Mark the ending point.
3. Run the function to show the elapsed time.

Look at the next code example to see these steps in action:

```
$this->benchmark->mark('start');
// something happens here
$this->benchmark->mark('end');
echo $this->benchmark->elapsed_time('start', 'end');
```

Here you can see the code in action. We mark the code start and end by using the same function, and simply echo out the returned value via the function `elapsed_time()`.

The names `start` and `end` are arbitrary, and can be anything you choose.

Setting multiple benchmarks

With the Benchmark Class, you can set multiple benchmarks and calculate the time difference between any of them, not just two. For example, we could set three benchmarks and time the difference between the first and second benchmark, and the first and third benchmark. We can use any combination of the benchmarks we set. Here's an example:

```
$this->benchmark->mark('tea');
// something happens here
$this->benchmark->mark('coffee');
// something else happens here
$this->benchmark->mark('biscuits');

echo $this->benchmark->elapsed_time('tea', 'coffee');
echo $this->benchmark->elapsed_time('coffee', 'biscuits');
echo $this->benchmark->elapsed_time('tea', 'biscuits');
```

As you can see from the example above, we can retrieve the time between two benchmark points even if there are one or more benchmarks between them.

Profiling your benchmarks

If you want your benchmarks to be available to the Profiler Class then you will need to set your benchmarks up in pairs. These pairs should end with **_start** and **_end**, but be otherwise identically named. See the next example:

```
$this->benchmark->mark('first_mark_start'):
// something happens
$this->benchmark->mark('first_mark_end');
$this->benchmark->mark('second_mark_start');
// something else happens
$this->benchmark->mark('second_mark_end');
```

Making use of the Profiler Class

As the Profiler Class is very small, we'll go over it here. The Profiler Class will output all benchmark results, queries you have run, and `$_POST` data at the bottom of your pages. The class will be automatically instantiated by the Output class as long as it is enabled. To enable the Profiler, you should place the following line of code anywhere in your Controller:

```
$this->output->enable_profiler(TRUE);
```

Once enabled, a report will be output at the bottom of your pages. Below is an example of what the profiler information looks like.

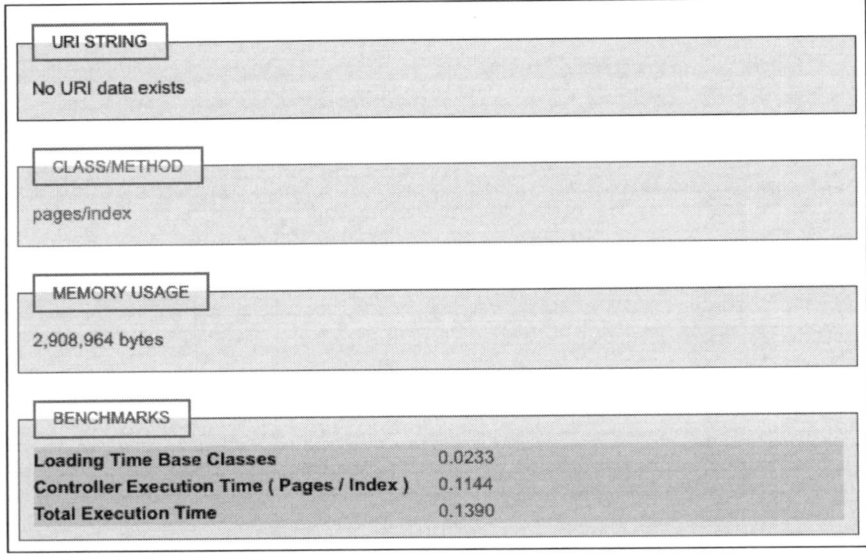

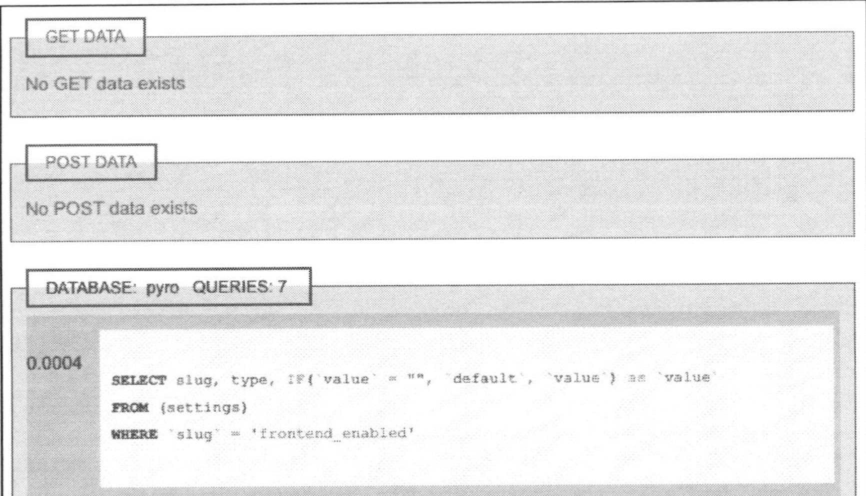

To disable the profiler, simply place the following code anywhere in your Controller:

```
$this->output->enable_profiler(FALSE);
```

Display total execution time

If you would like to display the total execution time for your application, simply place the following line of code anywhere in one of your view files:

```
<?php echo $this->benchmark->elapsed_time(); ?>
```

You may notice that this is the same function as when calculating the time between two benchmark points; except in this case we do not pass any parameters to the function. When no parameters are passed, the benchmark class simply runs and outputs the total execution time. Another, shorter way of displaying this data is to use the following line of code:

```
{elapsed_time}
```

The above is a pseudo-variable and is provided for developers who do not wish to use pure PHP in their View files.

Display memory consumption

If your PHP installation is configured with the option `-enable-memory-limit`, you can display the amount of memory used by the system by including the following line of code in your application:

```
<?php echo $this->benchmark->memory_usage(); ?>
```

This function can only be used in your View files. The memory consumption shown will be of the entire CodeIgniter application, not of two benchmarked points. Another way to show your memory consumption is to use the following pseudo-variable:

```
{memory_usage}
```

That's all you need to know in order to be able to use the CodeIgniter Benchmark Class. This is one of the simpler libraries that CodeIgniter offers, but is possibly one of the most underused, as well. Benchmarks offer a great way to monitor your application's speed, and greatly help developers who are building large-scale applications.

Input and Security Class

The Input and Security Class sanitizes all global data and filters all POST and COOKIE data to ensure that only alphanumeric characters are present. We've already used this class when we built our contact form, but there are a few things that we didn't cover.

XSS filtering

The Input and Security Class comes with a Cross Site Scripting hack prevention filter, which can be run on a per-item basis, or can be set to filter all POST and COOKIE data automatically. It is not set to run by default because it has a small processing overhead and is not always needed in every case.

The XSS filter works by looking for JavaScript that can be run on the page to hijack cookies or in other cases with malicious intent. All XSS found will be rendered safe by converting it into HTML entities.

Filtering a single item

This is mainly a recap: To filter POST or COOKIE data for Cross Site Scripting exploits, you run the data through the filter as shown:

```
$name = $this->input->xss_filter($this->input->post('name'));
```

In this instance, I took the value of the name field of an imaginary form. It can be the name of any form field that you like.

Automatic filtering

You can turn on XSS filtering all of the time and filter everything that comes through the library by changing the following line in the `system/application/config/config.php` file from:

```
$config['global_xss_filtering'] = FALSE;
```

to:

```
$config['global_xss_filtering'] = TRUE;
```

Filtering images

To ensure file upload security, there is an optional second parameter to the XSS clean function: **is_image**. This is used to check images for XSS attacks. When the second parameter is set to TRUE, the function returns TRUE if the image is safe, and FALSE if it is not, instead of simply returning an altered string.

Retrieving POST data

To retrieve post data, you should use the function shown next. The first parameter is the name of the POST item that you are looking for.

```
$this->input->post('some_field');
```

This function returns the item it if exists, and returns FALSE if it does not. The second function lets you run the data through the XSS filter without writing any more code. This is an easier way of running the XSS filter on a per-item basis.

```
$this->input->post('some_field', TRUE);
```

Retrieving GET data

The function for retrieving GET data is identical to the POST function, except that it only retrieves GET data.

```
$this->input->get('some_field', TRUE);
```

Retrieving GET and POST data

This function will search through the GET and POST streams for data; looking inside POST first, then GET. It works in the same way as the previous functions.

```
$this->input->get_post('some_field', TRUE);
```

Retrieving COOKIE data

This function is the same as those listed previously, but will only look in the COOKIE data.

```
$this->input->cookie('some_field', TRUE);
```

Retrieving SERVER data

This function is the same as the previous examples, except it only returns SERVER data.

```
$this->input->server('some_field', TRUE);
```

IP Addresses

To retrieve the user's IP address, you should use the next function. If the IP address isn't valid, it will return 0.0.0.0.

```
$this->input->ip_address();
```

To validate an IP address, you should use the next function. It will return TRUE or FALSE. The previous function validates the IP automatically.

```
if ( ! $this->input->valid_ip($ip))
{
  echo "Not a valid IP";
}
else
{
  echo "Valid IP!";
}
```

Retrieving a user agent

To determine the user agent of the user, you would use the next line of code. This will return the user agent of the user's web browser; if one isn't available it will return FALSE.

```
echo $this->input->user_agent();
```

Email Class

The Email Class is a CodeIgniter gem. It enables you to easily send e-mails from your application; this is great for simple contact forms, and even mailing lists for handling thousands of e-mails. The Email Class also serves as a wrapper class. This means that you can change the way that e-mails are sent, without having to change any of your Controller's code. You can choose between the standard PHP mail function, sendmail, or even Simple Mail Transfer Protocol (SMTP).

Send an e-mail

To get us started with the Email Class, we'll simply send an e-mail using the PHP mail function, which is also the default option for this library. To start using the library, you need to load it in the same way as you would any other library.

```
$this->load->library('email');
```

The next thing that we will need to do is to set our e-mail parameters, the sender, the recipient, any e-mail address to send a carbon copy or blind carbon copy to, the subject of our e-mail, and the message body. Take a look at the following code and see if you can distinguish the different parts of our e-mail:

```
$this->email->from('you@example.com', 'Your Name');
$this->email->to('someone@example.com');
$this->email->cc('another@person.com');
$this->email->bcc('theboss@example.com');

$this->email->subject('Email Test');
$this->email->message('This is a simple test we wrote for the email
class.');
```

Hopefully you can read the previous code example pretty easily. This is one of the benefits of CodeIgniter and its libraries. It's very easy to read CodeIgniter code. In the first line of code we set our e-mail address, which is the address that we will send the e-mail from, and also pass along a name to identify ourselves. In the next line, we set the recipient, who is the person that we are sending the e-mail to. The next line down is an e-mail address to send a carbon copy of the e-mail to. A carbon copy is simply a copy of the e-mail, just sent to another person. The final line of the first block is the e-mail address to which we will send a blind carbon copy to. A blind carbon copy is the same as a carbon copy, except for the other recipients of the e-mail do not know that this person also has received a copy of this e-mail.

We don't need to supply a CC and BCC e-mail for all of our e-mails; we're just covering it here so that you know that the library supports these extra e-mail parameters.

Now, to send our e-mail we simply call the `send` function of the e-mail library. Here's how we do it.

```
$this->email->send();
```

There is another function available to us from this library. It's a debugger that echo's out some information provided to us by the various mail sending protocols, and we are also notified what has been sent and whether or not the e-mail was sent successfully. To show the debugging information, we use the following line of code:

```
echo $this->email->print_debugger();
```

Our final code looks like this:

```
$this->load->library('email');
$this->email->from('you@example.com', 'Your Name');
$this->email->to('someone@example.com');
$this->email->cc('another@person.com');
$this->email->bcc('theboss@example.com');

$this->email->subject('Email Test');
$this->email->message('This is a simple test we wrote for the email
class.');

$this->email->send();
echo $this->email->print_debugger();
```

You are not just limited to sending e-mail from inside Controllers; e-mails can also be sent from Models.

Build a contact form

Before we go ahead and build our contact form, we need to specify what resources we need to create a usable contact from. The first thing is a contact form, which will be a view file, and will simply contain our form and echo out any errors that may occur. For this, we create a file inside the `system/application/views/` folder, called `email.php`.

Now we'll also need a Controller so that we can access and process our contact form. Create a file inside the `system/application/controllers/` folder, called `email.php`.

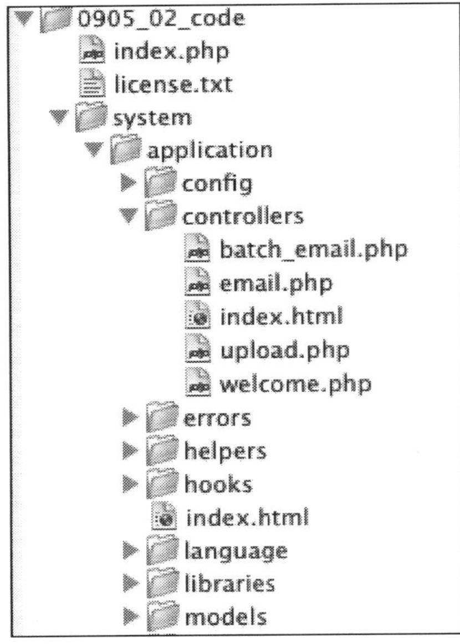

Our contact form

Our contact form will be very simple. All it will display is a message that we will pass to the view file (if one is provided), input boxes in which the user can enter their name, e-mail, and subject, and a text area for the message. This book assumes knowledge of HTML, so this file should be easy to understand.

```
<?php

if(isset($msg))
{
  echo $msg;
}

?>
<form method="POST">
Name<br />
<input type="text" name="name" /><br />

Email<br />
<input type="text" name="email" /><br />

Subject<br />
<input type="text" name="subject" /><br />
Message<br />
<textarea rows="17" cols="70" name="message"></textarea><br />

<input type="submit" name="contact" value="Send Email" />
</form>
```

Here's what the form looks like in the browser:

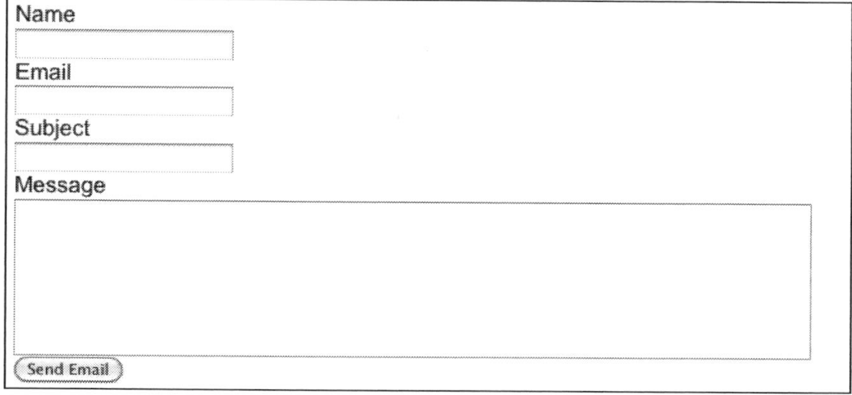

The Controller code will be much more complex. Before we dive into writing the code, we need to know what security measures we can put in place to ensure that this contact form is as secure as possible.

Firstly, we need to check that the form has been submitted; if it hasn't then we'll display the form. If it has been submitted then we'll process the data supplied from the form.

Secondly, we'll need to check that all of the fields are filled with data; we don't want any of the fields to be empty. If they are empty, we may be sending ourselves blank e-mails.

Also, we'll make sure that the e-mail provided is correctly formatted, so that we can e-mail the user back when we need to. This will be very easy, as we'll use the e-mail helper for this.

Finally we'll run all of the form fields through CodeIgniter's XSS filter, removing any code from the form and protecting our site against other types of vulnerability.

But before all that, we will load the Email Library and the Email Helper. The following two lines of code do exactly that. To send e-mails, we only need to use the Email Library; we load the Email Helper to easily validate any e-mail address we get from the user as a reply-to e-mail address. We can also use this library to send an e-mail with a single function.

```
$this->load->library('email');
$this->load->helper('email');
```

Checking if the form has been submitted

The first thing that we need to do is to check if the form has been submitted. We will do this by using the CodeIgniter Input Class. In brief, the Input Class destroys all global data not utilized by CodeIgniter, filters POST and COOKIE data, and provides an XSS filter. Here's the code that we need in order to check if the form has been submitted or not:

```
if($this->input->post('contact'))
{
  // process data here
}
else
{
  $this->load->view('contact');
}
```

The first line of code checks that the submit button has a value; this means the form has been submitted. If the form has been submitted then we will process the data (this part will come in a minute) but if not, then we'll simply load the form view file.

Checking the values of the form

We need to ensure that all of the form fields have been filled in. We can do this by simply using the `empty()` PHP function.

Before we do this, we want to assign the value of the form fields to variables. This makes it easy for us by saving us from having to type out `$this->input->post('name')` every time. Here's the code for this; it should be placed inside the `if` statement where the comment `// process data here` was.

```
$name = $this->input->post('name');
$email = $this->input->post('email');
$subject = $this->input->post('subject');
$message = $this->input->post('message');
```

With that out of the way, we can check to see if any of the fields were left blank, and show an error if they were.

```
if(empty($name) OR empty($email) OR empty($subject) OR
empty($message))
{
  show_404("The form submitted left fields blank, all fields are
required. Please go back and fill in all of the fields.");
}
```

Let me explain this code. What we do in the `if` statement is say "**If the name is empty, or the email is empty, or the subject is empty or the message is empty: show this error**". I've used `OR` in place of `||` in this instance as it's more readable, and is recommended by the CodeIgniter Style Guide.

Validate the e-mail

The next step that we need to take is to ensure that the email is correctly formatted. The Email Helper gives us an easy solution. It contains a function that checks whether a string is in the format `name@domain.ext`. Here's how we check the e-mail:

```
if(!valid_email($email))
{
  show_404("The email address provided is not a valid email. Please go
back and fill in all of the fields.");
}
```

Because of the way that I have coded it, I'm actually checking to see if the email is NOT valid, so I don't need an `else` statement. We simple use the function `valid_email()` provided by the Email Helper, by passing the e-mail to it. It will return TRUE or FALSE depending on whether the e-mail is valid or not.

Using the XSS filter

The final step to our security check is to pass all of the field data through the XSS filter. We could do this automatically, but I want to show you how to do it manually. All that we need to do is to pass the data to the function `$this->input->xss_clean()`, in order to ensure that everything is secure. Here's how we do that:

```
$name = $this->input->xss_clean($name);
$email = $this->input->xss_clean($email);
$subject = $this->input->xss_clean($subject);
$message = $this->input->xss_clean($message);
```

All that we do is to assign the variables the value of the cleaned variables from the XSS filter.

Send the e-mail

Finally, we can send our email! I'll cover two ways of sending an e-mail. The first way uses the Email Class, and the second way uses the Email Helper.

Using the Email Class

I covered how to send an e-mail using the Email class at the beginning of this section, except that in this case, I'll be using the data from the form.

```
$this->email->from($email, $name);
$this->email->to('youremail@yourdomain.ext');

$this->email->subject($subject);
$this->email->message($message);

$this->email->send();
```

There are a few differences this time around. To set the `from` e-mail address, I passed the e-mail to the first parameter of the `from()` function and the name to the second. The `to` e-mail address should be set to your e-mail. The subject and message are self-explanatory. Both have only one parameter: the subject or the e-mail message, respectively.

Finally the last line of code sends the e-mail.

Using the Email Helper

The Email Helper gives us a much simpler way of sending e-mails. We can do it with one line of code:

```
send_email('youremail@yourdomain.ext', $subject, $message);
```

There are a few down-sides to this solution, though. If you want to send both the user's e-mail and name, you'd need to concatenate them in either the subject or the message. The function is basically a wrapper for the PHP `mail()` function. If the native PHP function were to change slightly, you'd have to wait a short period for it to be updated in the Email Helper as well.

Batch e-mail processing

Batch email processing is great for users who want to have a mailing list with a large amount of users subscribed to it. What batch processing does is break up the emails into smaller chunks, so instead of sending 10,000 emails all at once, it would send 200 (by default) at a time. To enable Batch Processing, we will initialize the Email Class with a configuration value. Here's the code:

```
$config['bcc_batch_mode'] = TRUE;
$config['bcc_batch_size'] = 500; // 200 by default

$this->email->initialize($config);
```

The first configuration value sets the batch mode to TRUE; this enables batch processing. The second configuration value sets the number of e-mails per batch; this is 200 by default. Then, the final line initializes the `config` values for the class to use.

Now when you send large amounts of e-mails using this class, they will be sent in batches of 500 (unless you leave it at the default 200).

Please take note that the batch processing will only work for BCC e-mails; so each email that you send to users should use the `bcc()` function rather than `to()` or `cc()`. For example:

```
$this->email->bcc('email@domain.ext');
```

File Uploading Class

The File Uploading Class provides a simple way to upload files to your web server. It lets you easily change the types of files that can be uploaded and the maximum file size, and also gives you a few different preferences for file names.

Uploading files using this class is very simple, and usually the process of uploading a file will look something like this:

- The user is shown a form, and selects a file to upload
- The file is then validated to ensure that it meets your preferences
- If the file meets your preferences, then the file will be uploaded to the directory that you specify
- The user will be shown either a success message or an error message if the file doesn't meet the preferences that you set

Before we can create our Upload utility, we need to create an upload folder. Create a new folder in the `system/application/` folder, and call it `uploads`. If you are on a web server, you will need to CHMOD this directory to 777.

Create the Upload Views

Our upload form is going to be very simple; we'll just have one field – the upload field. We'll open the form by using the form helper because it's easier this way, and we can easily set the action to a Controller. So, create a file inside the `system/application/views/` folder, called `upload_form.php`, and type the following code into it:

```
<?php echo $error;?>

<?php echo form_open_multipart('upload/do_upload');?>

  File:<br />
  <input name="file" type="file" /><br />

  <input type="submit" name="submit" value="Upload" />
<?php echo form_close(); ?>
```

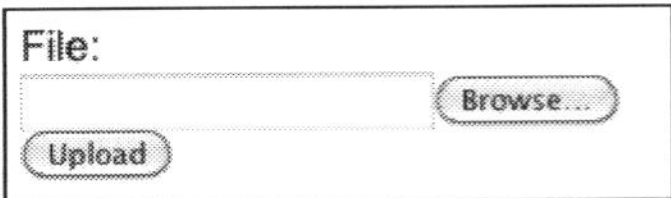

On the first line you'll notice that we're echoing out a variable. This is where we echo out any errors provided by the File Upload Class. This will also allow users to select a file that meets the requirements that we set.

We'll also need a view file showing the user a success message and the details of their file. We'll also add a link so that the user can choose to upload another file. You should name this file `upload_success.php`.

```
<h3>Your file was successfully uploaded!</h3>

<ul>
<?php foreach($upload_data as $item => $value):?>
<li><?php echo $item;?>: <?php echo $value;?></li>
<?php endforeach; ?>
</ul>

<p><?php echo anchor('upload', 'Upload Another File!'); ?></p>
```

A quick note. We use a function called `anchor()` to create the link to upload another file. This function lets us easily create a link to a URI string, without needed to include the whole URL, making it much easier than simply including the HTML. We pass the URI string to the first parameter and the link text to the second parameter of the function.

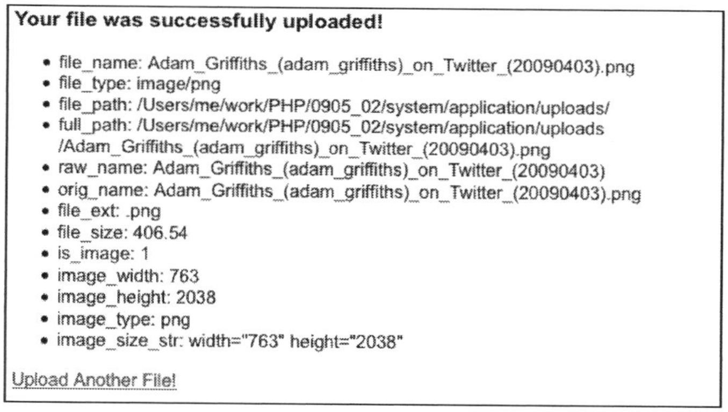

Your file was successfully uploaded!

- file_name: Adam_Griffiths_(adam_griffiths)_on_Twitter_(20090403).png
- file_type: image/png
- file_path: /Users/me/work/PHP/0905_02/system/application/uploads/
- full_path: /Users/me/work/PHP/0905_02/system/application/uploads /Adam_Griffiths_(adam_griffiths)_on_Twitter_(20090403).png
- raw_name: Adam_Griffiths_(adam_griffiths)_on_Twitter_(20090403)
- orig_name: Adam_Griffiths_(adam_griffiths)_on_Twitter_(20090403).png
- file_ext: .png
- file_size: 406.54
- is_image: 1
- image_width: 763
- image_height: 2038
- image_type: png
- image_size_str: width="763" height="2038"

Upload Another File!

The `foreach` loop I used here simply loops through all of the upload data provided by the Upload Class about the file, and echo's it out to the user. You probably wouldn't want to do this on a live website, but for our purposes it's good to learn from.

Create the Upload Controller

We need to create an Upload Controller to handle the uploading of the file and to complete all of our business logic. Here's a list of what the Controller will do:

- Load the necessary dependencies (libraries, helpers, and so on)
- Show the upload form to the user
- Specify the type of files that users can upload, and the maximum file size
- Validate the file to be uploaded
- Upload the file
- Show a success message

Now that we know what the Controller needs to do, we can decide on what types of files we'll allow users to upload. So let's build an image uploader. We'll allow GIF, JPEG, and PNG, and the images should be no larger than 1 MB. The reason behind defining this now is so that we can focus on the code later, rather than this, which can be worked out in this small planning phase.

Our initial controller

Here's our initial Controller; for now it just loads the dependencies that we need, shows our view file, and has an empty function for our upload process. We set the upload forms action to be `upload/do_upload` – this is simply a URI string and is why the function is named `do_upload`; we could set it to anything that we like if we wanted to.

```
<?php

class Upload extends Controller
{
  function Upload()
  {
    parent::Controller();
    $this->load->helper(array('form', 'url', 'file'));
  }

  function index()
  {
    $this->load->view('upload_form', array('error' => ' ' ));
  }
```

```
    function do_upload()
    {
    }

}
?>
```

Specify the allowed file types and maximum file size

The next thing we need to do is to specify the types of file and the maximum file size to the Upload Class. To do this, change the configuration values for the Upload Class, and initialize the class with the following edited values:

```
$config['upload_path'] = APPPATH . 'uploads/';
$config['allowed_types'] = 'jpeg|jpg|gif|png';
$config['max_size'] = '1024';
$this->load->library('upload', $config);
```

Uploading the file

The next task on our list is to validate the file. This is done in the same process as uploading the file, because the Upload Class makes it easy for us by providing a way to see if the file has been uploaded and easily see the errors if it hasn't.

```
$field_name = "file";

if ( ! $this->upload->do_upload($field_name))
{
  $error = array('error' => $this->upload->display_errors());

  $this->load->view('upload_form', $error);
}
else
{
  $data = array('upload_data' => $this->upload->data());

  $this->load->view('upload_success', $data);
}
```

The first thing that we do in this part of the code is initialize a variable with the value of the field name in the form for the uploaded file. Then we check to see if the value of the upload is invalid (that is, the upload hasn't completed); if this is the case then we show the errors above the upload form. If the file has been uploaded successfully, though, we grab the upload data and pass it through to the upload success view file.

Navigate to `http://yourwebsite.ext/index.php/upload/` and upload a few images. Try to upload a file type that isn't allowed and see what happens. This is a very simple uploader and can form the basis of a more complex system with a little more work.

Image Manipulation Library

Now that we've built ourselves a simple image uploader, we can take a look at the Image Manipulation Library. This class let's you create thumbnails, crop and resize images, rotate images, and even watermark images.

Watermarking images is only available using the GD or GD2 library. Although other libraries are supported, the GD library needs to be used for this process.

In order for most of the functions provided by this class to work, the image folder will need write permissions. In our case we have changed the permissions of the uploads folder to 777; this gives it read, write, and execute permissions, so we don't need to change anything else.

Initializing the library

Before using the Image Manipulation Library we need to set a few configuration values. We need to specify the image processing library to use (from GD, GD2, ImageMagick and NetPBM), the image that we are going to perform an action on, and a few more configuration values. We might also need to set some values if we are creating a thumbnail. Here's how we'd initialize the class to create a thumbnail:

```
$config['image_library'] = 'gd2';
$config['source_image'] = APPPATH . 'uploads/myimage.jpg';
$config['new_image'] = APPPATH . 'uploads/mynewimage.jpg';
$config['create_thumb'] = TRUE;
$config['maintain_ratio'] = TRUE;
$config['width'] = 75;
$config['height'] = 50;

$this->load->library('image_lib', $config);
```

On the first line, I set the image library to GD2; it's GD2 by default so it's there for teaching purposes. If you want to use GD2, you usually won't need to change it. The next line sets the source image—all you'd need to change here is the `myimage.jpg` filename, and the path is set correctly. We have also specified the name for the thumbnail image when we create it.

To create a thumbnail, you should set the `create_thumb` value to `TRUE`. You can also choose to maintain the ratio of the image and set the width and height.

The last line simply loads the library with the configuration values instead of the defaults.

Creating a thumbnail

Although we've set our configuration values to accommodate the creation of a thumbnail, we haven't actually done it yet. This is a very easy process, and only takes one function:

```
$this->image_lib->resize();
```

This resize function will simply resize the original image if `create_thumb` or `new_image` have been used. So make sure that you specify these values if you want to create a new thumbnail rather than change the uploaded image.

Cropping an image

Cropping an image using this library is also a painless operation. It requires two extra configuration values, to set the x and y values of where to crop the image.

```
$config['x_axis'] = '100';
$config['y_axis'] = '40';
```

You would then check to see if the function returns a success, and show the errors if it didn't complete.

```
if ( ! $this->image_lib->crop())
{
    echo $this->image_lib->display_errors();
}
```

It is very difficult to crop images without a visual representation of the image so this function is fairly useless unless you intend to build an interface to easily select the cropping area.

Here's a full example of cropping an image. Note that on line six we utilize the `initialize()` function. This lets us set up the library with different configuration values. This is useful if we need to make multiple calls to the same library for different tasks.

```
$config['image_library'] = 'gd2';
$config['source_image'] = APPPATH . 'uploads/myimage.jpg';
$config['x_axis'] = '100';
$config['y_axis'] = '60';

$this->image_lib->initialize($config);

if ( ! $this->image_lib->crop())
{
    echo $this->image_lib->display_errors();
}
```

Rotating an image

This function requires an additional configuration value to set the angle of rotation.

```
$config['rotation_angle'] = '90';
```

There are five available options for this value:

- 90 – rotates counter-clockwise 90 degrees
- 180 – rotates counter-clockwise 180 degrees
- 270 – rotates counter-clockwise 270 degrees
- hor – flips the image horizontally
- vrt – flips the image vertically

Here's a full example of rotating an image:

```
$config['image_library'] = 'gd2';
$config['source_image'] = APPPATH . 'uploads/myimage.jpg';
$config['x_axis'] = '100';
$config['y_axis'] = '60';

$this->image_lib->initialize($config);

if ( ! $this->image_lib->crop())
{
    echo $this->image_lib->display_errors();
}
```

Clearing values in loops

If you are looping through files, then you need to clear all of the values from the previous image. To do this you should add the following line of code at the end of the loop. This line must be included, or the image manipulation library will not process multiple images.

```
$this->image_lib->clear();
```

Pagination Class

Pagination refers to the system of numbering pages—a list of numbered links, usually found at the bottom of the page, which allow you to navigate to a different page. CodeIgniter's Pagination Class is easy to use and can be totally customized.

Example

Here's a simple example to show you how to use the Pagination Class in one of your Controllers:

```
$this->load->library('pagination');
$this->load->helper('url');

$config['base_url'] = site_url() . '/index.php/results/page/';
$config['total_rows'] = 200;
$config['per_page'] = 20;

$this->pagination->initialize($config);

echo $this->pagination->create_links();
```

This is all that you need in order to create paginated links. The library comes with around 20 configurable items, but you only need the three used previously to create the links.

The **base_url** is the URL of your controller. We used a function from the URL `helper`, which substitutes in the site URL for us, so we only have to change it in one place (`config/config.php`) if we need to, and not in every instance. The URI shows that we use a Controller called **Results** in a function called **page**. The final URI item will be the page number; it is usually located in the third parameter (there is no need to include the page number in your base URL), but you can use URI routing to use a different structure.

The next item, **total_rows** is the number of rows you have in your database. Usually this will be the number of rows returned from your database query.

Finally, **per_page** is the number of results that you want to show per page. In this example, we're showing twenty items per page; this would result in ten pages overall.

Customizing the pagination

There are more items that you can add to the `$config` variable upon initializing the class. The following items change the way that the pagination is displayed:

```
$config['uri_segment'] = 3;
```

This specifies the URI segment which will contain the page number. The class sets this automatically, but you can change it if you need to.

```
$config['num_links'] = 2;
```

This specifies the number of links to show on each side of the current page.

Customize the "First" link

You can also customize the "First" link.

```
$config['first_link'] = 'First';
```

This will set the first link text to "First". You can set it to anything; some other examples might be "<<" or "1st".

```
$config['first_tag_open'] = '<div>';
$config['first_tag_close'] = '</div>';
```

You can also wrap this link with a tag. In this case, we're wrapping it up in a `div` tag, but you can use anything that you like.

Customize the "Last" link

This is used in the same way as the first link; simply rename your `config` items as shown below:

```
$config['last_link'] = 'Last';
$config['last_tag_open'] = '<div>';
$config['last_tag_close'] = '</div>';
```

Customize the "Next" link

To customize the "Next" link, you would once again use the `config` values in the same way mentioned previously. If you intend to use a > for the next link, you will need to use the HTML entities for it, **>**.

```
$config['next_link'] = '&gt;';
$config['next_tag_open'] = '<div>';
$config['next_tag_close'] = '</div>';
```

Customize the "Previous" link

As with all the other customizable items, there are three possibilities that can be used to change the way the previous link is shown.

```
$config['next_link'] = '&lt;';
$config['next_tag_open'] = '<div>';
$config['next_tag_close'] = '</div>';
```

Customize the "Current Page" link

You can customize the way in which the current page link is shown. There are two options. The first is the tag to put before the link, and the second is the tag to put after the link.

```
$config['cur_tag_open'] = '<b>';
$config['cur_tag_close'] = '</b>';
```

Customize the "Digit" link

The two tags below would be wrapped around the link for the numbered pages.

```
$config['num_tag_open'] = '<div>';
$config['num_tag_close'] = '</div>';
```

Session Class

The Session Class allows you to maintain a user's state as they browse your website. The Session Class stores data inside a cookie, which can optionally be encrypted. You are also able to store data inside a database for added security, as this means that the user's cookie must match the database record. By default only a cookie is used. If you enable the database option then you'll need to create a database table, by using the steps given next.

The Session class doesn't make use of native PHP sessions. It uses it's own variation that utilizes cookies for storing data. You can optionally use a database to store all custom information as well. More on that is provided later in this chapter.

Initializing the Session Class

Sessions typically run globally upon each page load, so the Session Class must either be initialized by one of your Controllers, or be autoloaded by using CodeIgniter's autoload feature.

Autoload the Session Class

If you wish to autload the session class, simply open up the `system/application/config/autoload.php` file and add `session` to the libraries array. This will then be loaded with each page load so you won't have to add any code to your Controller in order to load the library.

Manually load the Session Class

To load the Session Class manually, simply put the following line of code into any of your Controllers:

```
$this->load->library('session');
```

How do CodeIgniter sessions work?

Upon every page load, the Session Class will check to see if a current session is active for the particular user. If the session doesn't exist or has expired, it will be regenerated. If a session does exist, its information will be updated. Every time the page is loaded, the user will be given a new session ID.

Once the Session Class is loaded, it will run automatically. You do not need to do anything to get the above operations to happen. You can work with the session data, and even add your own data to the session, but everything else is done automatically.

What is stored in a session?

A CodeIgniter session is simply an array containing the following data:

- The user's unique Session ID (this is a randomly-generated number, which is hashed with MD5 for portability, and is regenerated every five minutes)
- The user's IP address
- The user's User Agent string
- The "last activity" timestamp

This data is stored in a cookie as a serialized array. Take a look at this example:

```
[array]
(
     'session_id'     => random hash,
     'ip_address'     => 'string - user IP address',
     'user_agent'     => 'string - user agent data',
     'last_activity'  => timestamp
)
```

You can enable encryption on the cookie so that the array will be encrypted before being stored in the cookie. This makes the data highly secure and reduces the chances of people being able to edit their session cookie.

Adding session data

As I noted earlier, you are able to add your own custom session data. This allows you to store much needed information, such as whether or not a user is authenticated, quickly. To add data to the session array, you would use the code given next:

```
$data = array(
                'username'  => 'joebloggs',
                'email'     => 'j.bloggs@jbloggs.com',
                'logged_in' => TRUE
           );

$this->session->set_userdata($data);
```

This will add another three items to the session array: `username`, `email` and `logged_in`. If you wish to add session data one item at a time, the function also supports this syntax:

```
$this->session->set_userdata('item_name', 'item_value');
```

> Cookies can only store 4KB of data, so please be aware of this when storing data. If you have turned on encryption this will make the string substantially longer than normal.
>
> If you are storing session data in a database table too, custom data will only be stored in the database so this won't be a concern, as only the default session data will be stored in the cookie, and not all of the data.

Retrieving session data

So now you've stored your custom session data, you'll need to know how to retrieve it! To return the session data on a per-item basis you simply use the following code:

```
$this->session->userdata('item');
```

where `item` is the item name of the data that you stored. Let's keep going with the user authentication notion, and retrieve the username.

```
$username = $this->session->userdata('username');
```

If the item that you are trying to retrieve doesn't exist, then the function will return FALSE.

Hopefully this clears up exactly how to use this function.

Removing session data

It's likely that at some point during your applications life span you will want to remove some or all of the session data that you previously set. This can be done in two ways: removing a session item or multiple session items, or destroying the session.

Removing a single session item

To remove a single session item—the username, for example—you would use the following function:

```
$this->session->unset_userdata('username');
```

This is used in much the same way as retrieving an item: simply pass the name of the item to the first parameter of the function, and it will be removed.

Removing multiple session items

If you wish to remove a number of items from the session data, then you would pass an array to the first parameter. Take a look at the following example:

```
$items = array('username' => '', 'email' => '');

$this->session->unset_userdata($items);
```

This will remove the username and email address from the session data.

Destroying a session

To destroy a session completely, you would use the following function:

```
$this->session->sess_destroy();
```

This function should be called last, as it will destroy the session. If you use the Session Class for user authentication, this will essentially log the user out.

Flash data

CodeIgniter supports **flashdata** – data that is only available for one server request, and is then removed. Flash data is very useful, and is usually used for informational messages such as "You have been logged out" or "Removed user account".

Flash variables are prefixed with **flash_**, so avoid using this prefix for your own custom session data.

Add flashdata

Adding flashdata is much like adding custom session data. Take a look at the following example:

```
$this->session->set_flashdata('item', 'value');
```

You can also send an array to this function, exactly as you would when adding custom session data.

Read flashdata

Reading flashdata is done in the same way as reading normal session data; the only difference is the function used.

```
$this->session->flashdata('item');
```

Keep flashdata

If you need to keep flashdata active for an additional request, you should do so by using the following function:

```
$this->session->keep_flashdata('item');
```

Using a session database

As an added layer of security, you can store session data inside a database. This is great for applications that require a higher level of security, because it offers a way to validate the session data stored in the cookie.

When the session data is stored in a database, every time that a valid cookie is found a database query will be made to match it. If the session ID does not match, then the session is destroyed. Session ID's can never be updated; they can only be regenerated when a new session is created.

To store session data in a database you need to create a table. Here's a basic MySQL SQL query, taken from the CodeIgniter User Guide.

```
CREATE TABLE IF NOT EXISTS 'ci_sessions' (
session_id varchar(40) DEFAULT '0' NOT NULL,
ip_address varchar(16) DEFAULT '0' NOT NULL,
user_agent varchar(50) NOT NULL,
last_activity int(10) unsigned DEFAULT 0 NOT NULL,
user_data text NOT NULL,
PRIMARY KEY (session_id)
);
```

You also need to change a configuration value in order to enable the database option.

Open up the `system/application/config/config.php` file, and find the following line:

```
$config['sess_use_database'] = FALSE;
```

Change it to:

```
$config['sess_use_database'] = TRUE;
```

If youe table name is something other than `ci_session`, then you can rename it by changing another `config` value:

```
$config['sess_table_name'] = ci_session';
```

Simply change the value of the variable to the name of your session database. Here's what the block of code looks like:

```
/*
|--------------------------------------------------------------------------
| Session Variables
|--------------------------------------------------------------------------
|
| 'session_cookie_name' = the name you want for the cookie
| 'encrypt_sess_cookie' = TRUE/FALSE (boolean).  Whether to encrypt the cookie
| 'session_expiration'  = the number of SECONDS you want the session to last.
|  by default sessions last 7200 seconds (two hours).  Set to zero for no expiration.
| 'time_to_update'      = how many seconds between CI refreshing Session Information
|
*/
$config['sess_cookie_name']      = 'ci_session';
$config['sess_expiration']       = 7200;
$config['sess_encrypt_cookie']   = FALSE;
$config['sess_use_database']     = FALSE;
$config['sess_table_name']       = 'ci_sessions';
$config['sess_match_ip']         = FALSE;
$config['sess_match_useragent']  = TRUE;
$config['sess_time_to_update']   = 300;
```

Unit testing a class

Unit testing is the process of writing a test for each function in your application. Ideally, each test case is independent from all of the other tests.

Initializing the class

The Unit Testing Class is loaded in the same way as all of the CodeIgniter classes: by using the **$this->load->library** function.

```
$this->load->library('unit_test');
```

Once loaded, the class will be available by using **$this->unit**.

Running tests

Running a test involves supplying a test, an expected result, and a name for the test. You do not need to name your tests—this is optional, but is highly recommended if you have multiple tests.

Here's an example test:

```
$test = 1 + 1;
$expected_result = 2;
$test_name = "One add one";

$this->unit->run($test, $expected_result, $test_name);
```

This is a very simple example of a test, and hopefully gives you an understanding of how tests work.

If you were to test the return value of a function, you would do it like this:

```
$test = function_name();
$expected_result = 2;

$this->unit->run($test, $expected_result);
```

This would then compare the value returned from the function with the expected result. The results do not have to be numbers; I've used numbers here for simplicity.

Expected results should either be a literal match or a data type match. Here's an example of a literal match:

```
$this->unit->run('test', 'test');
```

Here is an example of a data type match:

```
$this->unit->run('test', 'is_string');
```

The value of the second parameter – **is_string** – will evaluate whether the test is a string or not. Here's a list of supported comparison types:

- is_string
- is_bool
- is_true
- is_false
- is_int
- is_numeric
- is_float
- is_double
- is_array
- is_null

Generating reports

You can generate reports after each test, or you can see a report of all tests at the end. To show a single report, simply echo out the **run** function.

```
echo $this->unit->run($test, $expected_result, $test_name);
```

To see a full report of all tests, use this function:

```
echo $this->unit->report();
```

The report will generate an HTML table for viewing. If you prefer to see raw data, you can by using the following function:

```
echo $this->unit->result();
```

Strict mode

By default, the Unit Testing Class will evaluate literal matches loosely. Take this example test:

```
$this->unit->run(1, TRUE):
```

This test is evaluating an integer, but the expected result is a Boolean. Due to PHP's loose data typing, the previous code will be evaluated as TRUE. Take the following raw PHP test as an example:

```
if (1 == TRUE) echo 'This evaluates as TRUE';
```

If you put the Unit Testing Class into strict mode, it essentially does this.

```
if (1 === TRUE) echo 'This evaluates as FALSE';
```

You can enable strict mode as follows:

```
$this->unit->use_strict(TRUE);
```

Enabling or disabling unit testing

If you would like to leave your tests in place in your scripts but do not want them to be run unless you need them to be run, you can disable unit testing with the following function:

```
$this->unit->active(FALSE);
```

Simply set it back to TRUE if you want to run the tests again:

```
$this->unit->active(TRUE);
```

Create a template

If you want the Unit Testing Class to format the final report differently from the default layout, you can set a different template, as follows:

```
$str = ''
<table border="0" cellpadding="4" cellspacing="1">
    {rows}
<tr>
<td>{item}</td>
<td>{result}</td>
</tr>
    {/rows}
</table>';

$this->unit->set_template($str);
```

Take note of the required pseudo-variables.

The template must be set before running the unit test process.

Summary

This chapter has taught you all you need to know in order to ensure that your application runs smoothly, by running benchmarks and unit tests, staying secure, using the input class, the security class, and the session class for secure authentication—and has also shown you how to build smaller applications such as a contact form and image uploader.

This is only a small part of CodeIgniter, and over the next two chapters you'll learn how to create secure forms and how to utilize CodeIgniter's awesome Database Library.

3
Form Validation and Database Interaction

Form validation is an important part of any application. Take a look at your favorite web application, notice that there are many forms in these web apps, and it is important that they be secure. It is also important that you have rules that should be adhered to; this also helps to keep a layer of security.

CodeIgniter's Form Validation Library gives you a great way to easily validate and secure your forms.

In this chapter you will:

- Learn how the form validation process works
- Build a contact form
- Apply validation rules to the form's input fields
- Use callbacks to create your own rules
- Perform database queries with the database library
- Return query results using the database helper functions
- Create queries using the active record library
- Learn how to cache active record queries
- Modify database tables using database forge

Why should I validate my forms?

The answer to this question is simple: security. If you simply left your forms bare, with no validation, and then stored this information directly in a database, you are liable to attack. People can simply place in some SQL code and can see a dump of a part or all of your database.

By using form validation and creating rules, you will disallow most, if not all, of these practices from occurring. By having set validation rules you can limit the types of data being allowed in your forms. Best of all, the Form Validation Library makes it easy to re-populate your form fields and to show individual errors for each field, making the overall end user experience better; which can mean a lot in an environment with many forms.

Even if you are building a contact form, it is a good idea to validate your forms to stop people abusing your form.

Using the Form Validation Library

In this chapter, we'll go back over the Contact Form we built in *Chapter 2, Learning the Libraries*, but we'll use the Form Validation Library instead of our own methods.

The form validation process

The Form Validation processes are different for the developers and for users. Read on to see how the user interacts with the forms, as well as how the developer will create the forms.

The user's process

A form is displayed to the user, who then fills it in and submits it. The Form Validation Library then checks the form against any rules that the developer has set. If an error occurs the library returns these errors and they are shown against the form with the fields re-populated. This process proceeds until a valid form is submitted.

The development process

You create a form, along with a dynamic value from a form helper function—this will re-populate the data if needed. You will also display individual or global errors in the form view file. You set validation rules, which must be adhered to. Then you check to see if the validation process has been run, and if it has not, you load the form view file.

Contact form

We previously validated the form data ourselves, checked when the form had been submitted, checked for empty fields, validated the e-mail, and then sent the e-mail off. In this chapter, we'll use the Form Validation Library to complete these tasks. All of the code shown should be in the `index()` function of your `email` controller.

Loading the assets

We need to load two libraries for our contact form: the Form Validation Library and the Email class. We can do this in one line, by passing an array to the `load->library` function.

```
$this->load->library(array('email', 'form_validation'));
```

We also need to load two helpers: the email helper and the form helper. We will do this in the same way as we loaded the two libraries in the previous line of code.

```
$this->load->helper(array('email', 'form'));
```

Setting the rules

The next step in using the Form Validation Library is to set the rules for the form. These rules are set and must be adhered to. The way we set rules is by using the `set_rules()` function of the Form Validation Library. We use the function as follows:

```
$this->form_validation->
  set_rules('field_name', 'human_name', 'rules');
```

As you can see, the function accepts three parameters. The first is the name of the form field that you wish to set the rule for. The second parameter is the name that you wish to be assigned to this, for humans to read. The final parameter is where you pass any validation rules.

List of validation rules

The following rules are readily available for use:

- required
- matches[field_name]
- min_length[x]
- max_length[x]
- exact_length[x]
- alpha

- alpha_numeric
- alpha_dash
- numeric
- integer
- is_natural
- is_natural_no_zero
- valid_email
- valid_emails
- valid_ip
- valid_base64

As you can see, some of these rules have a single parameter.

The rule `matches[]` will return TRUE if the field matches the field name passed to it.

The `min_length[]`, `max_length[]`, and `exact_length[]` rules will take an integer as a parameter and check if the minimum length, maximum length respectively, or exact length matches the rule.

The rules with no parameters are pretty much self-explanatory. You are able to use more than one rule, simply separate rules with a vertical bar '|' and they will cascade.

> These rules can also be called as discrete functions. You may also use any native PHP function that accepts one parameter as a rule.

```
$this->form_validation->required($string);
$this->form_validation->is_array($string); // native PHP function as a
                                            // rule
```

Prepping data

We can also use various prepping functions to prep the data before we apply rules to it. Here's a list of the prepping rules that we can perform:

- xss_clean
- prep_for_form
- prep_url
- strip_image_tags
- encode_php_tags

The first function listed is `xss_clean`. This basically strips out any code and unwanted characters, and replaces them with HTML entities.

The function `prep_for_form` will convert special characters so that HTML data can be shown in a form without breaking it.

The function `prep_url` will simply add `http://` to a URL, if it is missing.

The function `strip_image_tags` will remove image tags, leaving the RAW image URL.

The function `encode_php_tags` will convert PHP tags into entities.

You may also use any native PHP function that accepts one parameter as a rule.

The rules

Now that we know how to set rules and what the rules we can use are, we can go ahead and set the rules necessary for our form. All fields should be required, and the e-mail field should be validated to ensure that the e-mail address is correctly formatted. We also want to run all of the data through the XSS filter.

```
$this->form_validation->
  set_rules('name', 'Name', 'required|xss_clean');

$this->form_validation->
  set_rules('email', 'Email Address',
    'required|valid_email|xss_clean');

$this->form_validation->
  set_rules('subject', 'Subject', 'required|xss_clean');

$this->form_validation->
set_rules('message', 'Message', 'required|xss_clean');
```

Check the validation process

Instead of checking one of the form field's POST value to check if the form has been submitted, we simply check to see if the Form Validation Library has run. We do this by using the following code:

```
if($this->form_validation->run() === FALSE)
{
  // load the contact form
```

```
}
else
{
  // send the email
}
```

It's fairly simple: if the Form Validation Library hasn't processed a form, we display the form to the user; if the library has processed a form and there are no errors, we'll send the e-mail off.

Sending the email

As you'll notice, everything is the same as how we got the field data earlier.

```
$name = $this->input->post('name');
$email = $this->input->post('email');
$subject = $this->input->post('subject');
$message = $this->input->post('message');

$this->email->from($email, $name);
$this->email->to('youremail@yourdomain.ext');

$this->email->subject($subject);
$this->email->message($message);

$this->email->send();
```

Final controller code

Here is the entirety of our controller code:

```
<?php

class Email extends Controller
{
  function Email()
  {
    parent::Controller();
  } //  function Email()

  function index()
  {
    $this->load->library(array('email', 'form_validation'));
    $this->load->helper(array('email', 'form'));
```

```
    $this->form_validation->
      set_rules('name', 'Name', 'required|xss_clean');
    $this->form_validation->
      set_rules('email', 'Email Address',
        'required|valid_email|xss_clean');
    $this->form_validation->
      set_rules('subject', 'Subject', 'required|xss_clean');
    $this->form_validation->
      set_rules('message', 'Message', 'required|xss_clean');

    if($this->form_validation->run() == FALSE)
    {
      $this->load->view('email'); // load the contact form
    }
    else
    {
      $name = $this->input->post('name');
      $email = $this->input->post('email');
      $subject = $this->input->post('subject');
      $message = $this->input->post('message');

      $this->email->from($email, $name);
      $this->email->to('youremail@yourdomain.ext');

      $this->email->subject($subject);
      $this->email->message($message);
      $this->email->send();
    }
  } // function index()
} // class Email extends Controller

?>
```

Changes to the form view

There are a couple of changes that we need to make to the form view in order to get the data to re-populate, and to show any errors next to the form field.

Re-populating field values

This is a fairly simple process. If an error has occurred, all we need to do to get the field data to re-populate is to set the `value` attribute of our input box. We then set the value using a form helper function, `set_value()`. We pass the name of the form field to the first parameter of this function.

```
value="<?php echo set_value('name'); ?>"
```

Showing individual errors

To display the errors, we do the same as we did earlier, but this time we use a different function and place it below the input box. The function that we use this time is `form_error()`.

```
<?php echo form_error('name'); ?>
```

Final form view

Here is the complete code for our view file:

```
<?php echo form_open(); ?>

Name<br />
<input type="text" name="name"
  value="<?php echo set_value('name'); ?>" />
<?php echo form_error('name'); ?><br />

Email<br />
<input type="text" name="email"
  value="<?php echo set_value('email'); ?>" />
<?php echo form_error('email'); ?><br />

Subject<br />
<input type="text" name="subject"
  value="<?php echo set_value('subject'); ?>" />
<?php echo form_error('subject'); ?><br />

Message<br />
<textarea rows="17" cols="70" name="message">
  <?php echo set_value('message'); ?></textarea>
<?php echo form_error('message'); ?><br />

<input type="submit" name="contact" value="Send Email" />
<?php echo form_close(); ?>
```

The form should appear as follows:

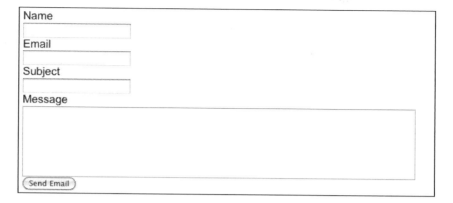

Changing the error delimiters

You can change the way that the errors are displayed to have them contained within custom HTML tags. This is useful for when you want to assign a CSS class in order to the errors to display them differently.

Changing delimiters globally

To change the error delimiters globally, add the next line of code after loading the Form Validation Library:

```
$this->form_validation->
  set_error_delimiters('<div class="error">', '</div>');
```

Changing delimiters individually

You can change the delimiters on a case-by-case basis. In the form view file change the way you show the errors by including two parameters in the errors function(s).

```
<?php

  echo form_error('field name', '<div class="error">', '</div>');

?>
```

You can also use:

```
<?php echo validation_errors('<div class="error">', '</div>'); ?>
```

Saving sets of validation rules to a config file

You can save sets of rules to a config file. To start, create a new file called `form_validation.php`, inside the `application/config/` directory. The rules must be contained within a variable `$config`, as with all other config files. The rules from our contact form would now appear as follows:

```
$config = array(
        array(
          'field' => 'name',
          'label' => 'Name',
          'rules' => 'required|xss_clean'
        ),
        array(
          'field' => 'email',
          'label' => 'Email Address',
          'rules' => 'required|valid_email|xss_clean'
        ),
        array(
          'field' => 'subject',
          'label' => 'Subject',
          'rules' => 'required|xss_clean'
        ),
        array(
          'field' => 'message',
          'label' => 'Message',
          'rules' => 'required|xss_clean'
        )
);
```

Creating sets of rules

If you have more than one form that needs validating, you can create sets of rules. To do this, you need to place the rules into 'sub-arrays'. The rules for our contact form would appear as follows when we place it into a set:

```
$config = array(
        'email' => array(
                      array(
                            'field' => 'name',
                            'label' => 'Name',
                            'rules' => 'required|xss_clean'
```

```
                        ),
                        array(
                                'field' => 'email',
                                'label' => 'Email Address',
                                'rules' =>
                                  'required|valid_email|xss_clean'
                        ),
                        array(
                                'field' => 'subject',
                                'label' => 'Subject',
                                'rules' => 'required|xss_clean'
                                ),
                        array(
                                'field' => 'message',
                                'label' => 'Message',
                                'rules' => 'required|xss_clean'
                                )
                    )
);
```

This method allows you to have as many sets of rules as you need.

Calling a specific set of rules

You need to specify the rule set that you want to validate the form against, on the `run` function. Our edited controller would now look like this:

```
if($this->form_validation->run('email') == FALSE)
{
  $this->load->view('email'); // load the contact form
}
else
{
  // send the email
}
```

Associating a rule group with a controller

You can use these groups to automatically associate them with a controller and function. This time, instead of calling the group `email`, we'll call it `email/index`—this will associate the rule group with the controller `email` and the function `index`.

```
$config = array(
            'email/index' =>
              array(
                array(
                       'field' => 'name',
                       'label' => 'Name',
                       'rules' => 'required|xss_clean'
                       ),
                array(
                       'field' => 'email',
                       'label' => 'Email Address',
                       'rules' => 'required|valid_email|xss_clean'
                       ),
                array(
                       'field' => 'subject',
                       'label' => 'Subject',
                       'rules' => 'required|xss_clean'
                       ),
                array(
                       'field' => 'message',
                       'label' => 'Message',
                       'rules' => 'required|xss_clean'
                       )
              )
);
```

This way, you won't need to explicitly say which rule group you want your form to be validated against.

Using callbacks

The Form Validation Library allows you to use callbacks as rules. A callback is simply a function in your Controller code that is used in place, or along with, a rule.

Say, for example, you want to add the user's e-mail address to the database if they haven't sent you an e-mail before. We can do this with a callback.

Firstly though, let's create the database table. There will be three fields: an ID, the user's name, and the user's e-mail address.

```
CREATE TABLE IF NOT EXISTS `user_data` (
  `id` INT( 11 ) NOT NULL AUTO_INCREMENT PRIMARY KEY ,
  `name` VARCHAR( 255 ) NOT NULL ,
  `email` VARCHAR( 255 ) NOT NULL
);
```

Include the callback in the rules

To add a callback into the rules, simply prefix the name of the function with `callback_`. Here is the rule for the e-mail field, again, with our callback added:

```
$this->form_validation->
  set_rules('email', 'Email Address',
    'required|valid_email|callback_add_user|xss_clean');
```

Here you can see that we've added the rule `callback_add_user`—this will run the e-mail through the function `add_user()` in our controller.

Creating the callback

To create the callback, first we need to decide how it will work.

Firstly, we will want to see if the e-mail already exists in the database; if so we won't do anything. If the e-mail isn't in the database, we'll add it along with the persons name.

Create the function

Creating a function is easy. A note about using callbacks, first. When using a callback, the Form Validation Library will pass the value of the field to the callback, so to get the e-mail into our callback we simply need to create a variable to retrieve it.

```
function add_user($email) { }
```

Load the database library

We'll need to load the database library. We do this slightly differently than other libraries, because it is larger than the others.

```
$this->load->database();
```

Performing the database query

There won't be lots of detail here, because the next chapter covers everything that you will need to know about the database library. To perform a basic SQL query, we use the following function:

```
$this->db->query();
```

So our code will look like this:

```
$query = $this->db->
  query("SELECT * FROM `user_data` WHERE `email` = '$email'");
```

Adding a condition

We only want to add the user's name and their e-mail address if the email doesn't exist already. To do this, we'll need to check to see if the number of rows returned from the query is zero.

To do this, we will use a helper function provided by the database library called `num_rows`.

```
if($query->num_rows() === 0)
{
  $name  = $this->input->post('name');

  $this->db->
    query("INSERT INTO `user_data` (name, email)
      VALUES ('$name', '$email')");
}
```

In this example we used an explicit comparison (===); we check that the value of the number of rows returned is identical to `0`. If we had used == then the result `FALSE` would run through the comparison as `TRUE` and the code in the loop would run when we didn't want it to.

You will also notice from this code that we are using the same function as we did to get the data from the database to insert the e-mail as well. The code inside the `if` statement will only be run if there is no previous record of the e-mail in the database.

Show a success page

To show the user that some progress has been made, let's add in the success page. Find the following line of code:

```
$this->email->send();
```

Add the following lines below it:

```
$data['msg'] = "Thank you, your email has now been sent.";
$this->load->view('email_success', $data);
```

Now, create a file inside the `system/application/views/` folder called `email_success.php` and add the following line of code into it.

```
<?php echo $msg; ?>
```

All we need to do is echo the variable out. You should, of course, add any layout code if you're using this on a live website, because at the moment, we simply display the message as seen in the next screenshot.

Thank you, your email has now been sent.

Database interaction

Databases are the backbone behind any Web application. Without a database, you'd have nowhere to hold all of your data, and SQL queries can become long and cumbersome to type out. Thankfully, CodeIgniter gives us a brilliantly simple way to interact with our Database. The database library also makes changing between database types—from MySQL to Oracle, for example—easier, because it acts as a wrapper and provides many functions for us to use on the database.

Loading the library

Loading the Database library is slightly different from loading other libraries. This is because it is large and resides in a different folder, unlike the other libraries.

```
$this->load->database();
```

Performing simple queries

Let's dive straight in by starting with the simple stuff. CodeIgniter gives us a function that we can pass a SQL Query to, and the query will be run on the database. Here's how it works:

```
$this->db->query('PUT YOUR SQL HERE');
```

This function is incredibly simple to use; you simply use this function in place of any native PHP functions you would use to run queries. This function will return TRUE or FALSE for write queries, and will return a dataset for read queries.

There is another function that you can use for very simple queries; this will only return TRUE or FALSE. It won't let you cache your query or run the query timer. In most cases you won't want to use this function.

```
$this->db->simple_query('PUT YOUR SQL HERE');
```

The SQL code that you pass to these functions are database-dependent. Only Active Record queries are independent of any type of Database SQL.

Returning values

You can assign the function `$this->db->query()` to a variable. You can then run a number of helper functions on the variable in order to return the data in different formats. Take the following example:

```
$query = $this->db->query('SELECT * FROM 'users'');
```

Returning a result object

In this case, returning the result will return an array of objects, or an empty array if the query failed. You would usually use this function in a `foreach` loop.

```
foreach($query->result() as $row)
{
  echo $row->username;
  echo $row->email;
}
```

If your query does not return a result, the CodeIgniter User Guide encourages you to check for a failure before using this function.

```
if($query->num_rows > 0)
{
  foreach($query->result() as $row)
   {
   echo $row->username;
   echo $row->email;
   }
}
```

Returning a result array

You are also able to return the result dataset as an array. Typically, you would use this function inside a `foreach` loop as well.

```
foreach($query->result_array() as $row)
{
  echo $row['username'];
  echo $row['email'];
}
```

Returning a row object

If your query is only expected to return a single result, you should return the row by using the following function. The row is returned as an object.

```
if($query->num_rows() > 0)
{
  $row = $query->row();

  echo $row->username;
  echo $row->email;
}
```

You can return a specific row by passing the row number as a digit in the first parameter.

```
$query->row(2);
```

Returning a row array

You can return a row as an array, if you prefer. The function is used in the same way as the previous example.

```
if($query->num_rows() > 0)
{
  $row = $query->row_array();

  echo $row['username'];
  echo $row['email'];
}
```

You can return a numbered row by passing the digit to the first parameter, also.

```
$query->row_array(2);
```

Result helper functions

Besides the helper function that helps to return the dataset in different ways, there are some other more generalized helper functions.

Number of rows returned

Used in the same way as the other helper functions, this will return the total number of rows returned from a query. Take the following example:

```
echo $query->num_rows();
```

Number of fields returned

Just like the previous function, this will return the number of fields returned by your query.

```
echo $query->num_fields();
```

Free result

This function will remove the resource ID associated with your query, and free the associated memory. PHP will usually do this by default, although when using many queries you may wish to use this to free up memory space.

```
$query->free_result();
```

Active Record

The Active Record in CodeIgniter is quite different to the AR you may find in Rails or other frameworks. The way that Active Record in CodeIgniter works is that you build up your queries using different functions. For simple queries, you might only need to use one or two functions, but for some you may need to use more—for example, if you have to look for certain conditionals, such as where a username and password are the same.

Selecting data

All of the functions in this section will build SQL `SELECT` queries. All of the SQL in this section is MySQL; other database systems may differ slightly.

$this->db->get();

The simplest query that you can do with Active Record is to select a full database table. This is done with one single function:

```
$this->db->get();
```

This would create the SQL query:

```
SELECT * FROM `table_name`
```

This function has three parameters. The first is the name of the database table. The second lets you set a limit, and the third lets you set an offset.

```
$query = $this->db->get('table_name', 10, 20);
```

This would then produce the SQL query:

```
SELECT * FROM `table_name` LIMIT 20, 10
```

$this->db->get_where();

This function works in much the same way as the previous function. The only difference is that the second parameter should be passed as an array. The array should have the name of the field and the value to use to fill in the `WHERE` part of your query.

```
$query = $this->db->get('table_name', array('id' => $id), 10, 20);
```

This would produce the following SQL query:

```
SELECT * FROM 'table_name' WHERE 'id' = $id LIMIT 10, 20
```

$this->db->select();

This function allows you to write the `SELECT` portion of your query. Take a look at the following example:

```
$this->db->select('name, username, email');
$query = $this->db->get('users');
```

The SQL query produced from this function will be:

```
SELECT name, username, email FROM `users`
```

You should take note that when using this function, and any of the other functions that let you write a portion of your query, that you still need to use the get() function to actually produce and run the query.

If you are selecting everything form your database (*) then you do not need to use this function as CodeIgniter assumes that you mean to select everything.

$this->db->from();

This function allows you to write the FROM portion of your query. This is basically the same as using the get() function, although it is slightly more readable. You can use whichever method you prefer.

```
$this->db->from('table_name');
$query = $this->db_>get();
```

$this->db->join();

This function lets you write the JOIN part of your query. Here's an example:

```
$this->db->select('*');
$this->db->from('blogs');
$this->db->join('comments', 'comments.id = blogs.id');

$query = $this->db->get();
```

You can specify a different type of join in the third parameter. You can choose from **left**, **right**, **outer**, **inner**, **left outer**, and **right outer**.

```
$this->db->join('comments', 'comments.id = blogs.id', 'left');
```

$this->db->where();

This function is used to build the WHERE portion of your query. This function can be used in a variety of ways.

Single key or value method

```
$this->db->where('name', $name);
```

This will produce the following SQL query. Note that the equals sign has been added for your convenience.

```
WHERE `name` = '$name'
```

Multiple key or value method

```
$this->db->where('name', $name);
$this->db->where('email', $email);
```

These two clauses will be appended to each other, and the word AND will be placed in between them.

Custom key or value method

You can include an operator in the first parameter, in order to change the default behavior (that is, using an = sign).

```
$this->db->where('name !=', $name);

// Produces WHERE `name` != '$name'
```

Associative array method

You can pass values to the `where()` function by using an associative array. Take a look at the following example:

```
$array = array('name' => $name, 'email' => $email);
$this->db->where($array);
```

You can include operators in the array, just as you would use in the first parameter.

```
$array = array('name !=' => $name, 'email' => $email);
$this->db->where($array);
```

Custom string

You can write your own custom WHERE clauses by passing a string to the first parameter.

```
$where = "name = 'Billy' AND job_title = 'MD'";
$this->db->where($where);
```

The `where()` function includes an optional third parameter. When set to FALSE, CodeIgniter will not try to protect your queries by adding backticks.

$this->db->like();

This function allows you to write the `LIKE` portion of your query, and functions in almost the exact same way as the `where()` method.

Single key or value method

This method is the same as the `where()` method, when used as follows:

```
$this->db->like('name', $name);
```

Multiple key or value method

This method is also the same as the `where()` method. Multiple calls will be chained together.

```
$this->db->like('name', $name);
$this->db->like('email', $email);
```

This function actually has three parameters. The first is the title of the field, the second is the match, and the third specifies where you want the wildcard to be placed. Your options are **before**, **after** and **both** (both is the default).

Associative array method

You can pass values to the `like()` function by using an associative array. Take a look at the following example:

```
$array = array('name' => $name, 'email' => $email);
$this->db->like($array);
```

$this->db->group_by();

This function lets you write the `GROUP BY` portion of your query.

```
$this->db->group_by('name');
$this->db->group_by(array('name', 'title'));
```

$this->db->order_by();

This lets you write the `ORDER BY` portion of your query. The first parameter is for your field name. The second is the type of order that you want to use, and can be **asc**, **desc**, or **random**.

Random sorting is not currently supported in Oracle or MSSQL Drivers. These will default to asc.

```
$this->db->order_by('name', 'desc');
```

You can also pass a string as the first parameter.

```
$this->db->order_by('name desc, title asc');
```

Multiple function calls can also be used, as for other functions.

```
$this->db->order_by('name', 'desc');
$this->db->order_by('title', 'asc');
```

$this->db->limit();

This function lets you add a LIMIT specification to your query. The first parameter will be the number to limit to, and the second parameter let's you set an offset.

```
$this->db->limit(10, 20);
```

Inserting data

Inserting data using Active Record is a very simple process, and there are just two functions that you may need to use in order to insert data into your database.

$this->db->insert();

This will generate an insert string based upon the data that you supply to it. The first parameter is the name of the table that you want to add the data to, and the second parameter can either be an array or an object of the data.

```
$data = array('name' => 'Bob Smith',
      'email' => 'bob@smith.com');

$this->db->insert('table_name', $data);
```

This would then produce the following SQL statement:

```
INSERT INTO mytable (name, email)
  VALUES ('Bob Smith', 'bob@smith.com')
```

All values will be properly escaped before being inserted into the database.

$this->db->set();

This function lets you set data for inserts or updates to your table. This can be used in place of passing an array of data to the `insert` or `update` function.

```
$this->db->set('name', 'Bob Smith');
$this->db->insert('table_name');
```

If you use multiple function calls they will be properly formatted, depending on whether you are performing an update or an insert.

This function also supports a third parameter. When set to FALSE, this third parameter will prevent data from being escaped.

You can also pass an associative array to this function.

```
$array = array('name' =>'Bob Smith', 'email' => 'bob@smith.com');

$this->db->set($array);
$this->db->insert('table_name');
```

Updating data

Updating data is a highly important part of any web application. CodeIgniter makes this really simple to do. The `update` function works in largely the same way as the `insert` function.

$this->db->update();

This will generate an update string based upon the data that you supply to it. The first parameter is the name of the table you want to add the data to, and the second parameter can either be an **array** or an **object** of the data. The third, optional parameter enables you to set the `WHERE` clause of your SQL query.

```
$data = array('name' => 'Bob Smith',
              'email' => 'bob@smith.com');

$this->db->where('id', 5);
$this->db->update('table_name', $data);
```

This would then produce the following SQL statement:

```
UPDATE mytable SET name = 'Bob Smith', email = 'bob@smith.com'
```

All values will be properly escaped before being inserted into the database.

You can optionally use the `where()` method to set the `WHERE` clause of the query. Here's how you would use the third parameter to set the `WHERE` clause:

```
$data = array('name' => 'Bob Smith',
              'email' => 'bob@smith.com');

$this->db->update('table_name', $data, 'id = 5');
```

Just as for inserting data, you may use the `set()` method in place of an array.

Deleting data

You can delete data from your tables in a variety of ways. You can either delete fields from a database or empty a database.

$this->db->delete();

This function accepts two parameters. The first is the name of the table, and the second should be an array from which to build the `WHERE` clause.

```
$this->db->delete('table_name', array('id' => 5));
```

You can also use the `where()` function to build the `WHERE` clause:

```
$this->db->where('id', 5);
$this->db->delete('table_name');
```

An array of table names can be passed into this function, if you wish to delete more than one table.

```
$tables = array('table1', 'table2', 'table3');
$this->db->where('id', '5');
$this->db->delete($tables);
```

$this->db->empty_table();

This function provides an easy way to delete all of the data from a table. Simply pass the name of the table to the first parameter, to empty it.

```
$this->db->empty_table('table_name');
```

$this->db->truncate();

This function will generate a `TRUNCATE` command and run it. It can be used in two ways:

```
$this->db->from('table_name');
$this->db->truncate();
```

or

```
$this->db->truncate('table_name');
```

Use whichever you feel more comfortable with, or the one that you find is most readable.

Active Record caching

Although the Active Record caching functionality provided by CodeIgniter is not true caching, it enables you to save a query for use later on in your script execution. Usually, an SQL query is reset after it has been completed. With Active Record caching you can prevent this reset and reuse queries easily.

The three caching functions available are listed next.

$this->db->start_cache();

This function must be called in order to begin the caching process. Not all queries can be cached. The cacheable queries are as follows:

- SELECT
- FROM
- JOIN
- WHERE
- LIKE
- GROUPBY
- HAVING
- ORDERBY
- SET

$this->db->stop_cache();

This function must be called in order to stop caching.

$this->db->flush_cache();

This function will delete all items from the Active Record cache.

Here's an example of Active Record caching:

```
$this->db->start_cache();
$this->db->select('field_1');
$this->db->stop_cache();

$this->db->get('tablename');

// Produces: SELECT `field_1` FROM (`tablename`)

$this->db->select('field_2');
$this->db->get('tablename');

// Produces: SELECT `field_1`, `field_2` FROM (`tablename`)

$this->db->flush_cache();

$this->db->select('field_2');
$this->db->get('tablename');

// Produces: SELECT `field_2` FROM (`tablename`)
```

Method chaining

Method chaining is available to everyone using PHP5. It enables you to vastly simplify your syntax by connecting multiple functions. Take a look at this example:

```
$this->db->select('name, email')->from('users')->
  where('id', 5)->limit(10, 20);
$query = $this->db->get();
```

This would produce the following SQL statement:

```
SELECT name, email FROM `users` WHERE `id` = 5 LIMIT 10, 20
```

Manipulating databases with Database Forge

The Database Forge class includes functions that enable you to perform operations on your databases and create new database schemas.

Loading the Forge class

Loading the Forge class is similar to loading the Database class.

```
$this->load->dbforge();
```

Once loaded, you can use all of the functions shown in this section.

Creating a database

Creating a database by using `dbforge` is fairly simple. It only takes a single function. The function will return TRUE or FALSE, depending upon the success or failure of the call.

```
if ($this->dbforge->create_database('my_db'))
{
    echo 'Database created!';
}
```

Dropping a database

Dropping a database is much like creating a database. It, too, only takes a single function, which returns TRUE or FALSE depending upon the success or failure of the call.

```
if ($this->dbforge->drop_database('my_db'))
{
    echo 'Database deleted!';
}
```

Adding fields

To add fields to your database table, you use the function `$this->dbforge->add_field();`. Once the fields have been defined, a call to the `create_table` function should be made.

You can add fields by using a multi-dimensional array. Here's an example:

```
$fields = array(
                'users' =>
                  array(
                        'type' => 'VARCHAR',
                        'constraint' => '100',
                  )
);
```

When adding a field like this, each defined field must have a 'type' key. This relates to the data type of the field. Some types require a constraint key. In this example the `VARCHAR` is limited to 100 characters.

Creating an ID field has it's own exception. To create an ID, you need to use the following function. ID fields are automatically assigned as an `INT(9) auto_incrementing Primary Key`.

```
$this->dbforge->add_field('id');
```

Creating a table

After fields and keys have been defined, you can create a table by using the following function:

```
$this->dbforge->create_table('table_name');
```

An optional second parameter will add `IF NOT EXISTS` when set to `TRUE`.

```
$this->dbforge->create_table('table_name', TRUE);
```

Dropping a table

Dropping a table is made very simple with the Forge Class. Just a single function is needed:

```
$this->dbforge->drop_table('table_name');
```

Renaming a table

Renaming a table takes one function. The first parameter is the old table name, and the second is the new table name.

```
$this->dbforge->rename_table('old_table_name', 'new_table_name');
```

Modifying a table

There are a few functions that you can use in order to modify a table. You can add, modify, and drop columns.

$this->dbforge->add_column();

This function accepts two parameters. The first is the name of the table that you wish to add to, and the second is an array of the columns that you wish to add.

```
$fields = array(
                'preferences' =>
                   array('type' => 'TEXT')
);
$this->dbforge->add_column('table_name', $fields);
```

$this->dbforge->drop_column();

This function is used to drop a column from a table. There are two parameters: the first should be the table name and the second should be the name of the table that you wish to drop.

```
$this->dbforge->drop_column('table_name', 'column_to_drop');
```

$this->dbforge->modify_column();

This function is identical to that of the `add_column` function, except that it renames the column.

```
$fields = array(
               'old_name' => array(
                                   'name' => 'new_name',
                                   'type' => 'TEXT',
                             ),
);
$this->dbforge->modify_column('table_name', $fields);
```

Summary

That's it. There you have it, you've now learned how to validate your forms and use the Database Library properly.

In the next chapter, we'll create a new library that allows us to handle User Authentication. The library we create will be fairly simple but will handle all logins and registration of new user accounts.

4

User Authentication 1

User authentication is an important part of any web application; it is also important that you know how to handle user authentication yourself, without relying on third-party sites such as Twitter and Facebook.

This chapter will show you:

- How to handle user registrations
- How to authenticate users by using a Model
- A real world example of the Form Validation Library

Defining our goals

Before we go ahead and jump into writing code, we need to define what we need to do. Setting goals before we write code is beneficial in three ways.

Firstly we will know all of the features that our code should have, and can limit ourselves to just that, which will eliminates scope creep (also known as feature creep).

Secondly, when given a set of goals, we can visualize how we will write the code in our heads. If you know what to expect at the end, you can build it much faster, because you will already know what it should look like.

Finally, once we finish writing our code we can go back and check if we have met all of our goals. This helps us to decide whether or not we were successful. If for some reason we did not meet a goal, we could consider it a failed project unless there is a good reason for this. For example, we could start writing a portion of code and realize that there is a better way of doing it. In this case, not meeting the goal would be a good thing. But this would not be the case in all of our projects. Goals are an important way to decide if an application is successful, and can help us to create better code and better projects in the future.

Our goals

We need to be able to handle user registrations and allow new users to sign up for an account. We'll have to ensure that the username they have chosen is available, and that the e-mail address isn't already being used for an existing account. This will help to prevent people from having multiple accounts.

We must use the Form Validation Library to handle all of our forms. This gives us two benefits:

- We can make use of callbacks to easily check if a username or email address is in use or not
- We can easily show form errors and repopulate the form data

We will be using a Model and a Controller to handle everything, instead of writing a Library. Sometimes Libraries can offer us some extra benefits; but in this case we don't need any benefits, we simply need to handle user accounts easily.

Creating and connecting to the database

Before we do anything, we need to create our database. Open up your favorite database editor and create a new database. Next, you should run the following SQL code to create the `users` table.

This SQL has only been tested with MySQL. Therefore it is advised that if you are using another database platform, you create the same table schema graphically or write your own SQL code.

```
CREATE TABLE `users` (
  `id` INT( 11 ) NOT NULL AUTO_INCREMENT PRIMARY KEY ,
  `username` VARCHAR( 255 ) NOT NULL ,
  `email` VARCHAR( 255 ) NOT NULL ,
  `password` VARCHAR( 255 ) NOT NULL
)

ENGINE = MYISAM;
```

Once that is done we need to edit our database configuration file. We do this by opening up `/system/application/config/database.php` and editing the following lines to correctly reflect our own details:

```
$db['default']['hostname'] = "localhost";
$db['default']['username'] = "";
$db['default']['password'] = "";
$db['default']['database'] = "";
$db['default']['dbdriver'] = "mysql";
```

If you are running on your local machine or a shared hosting account, it is likely that you won't need to change the `hostname` value. You must set the `username`, `password` and `database` values correctly, or CodeIgniter will not be able to connect to the database when needed, and will display an error message. With all of that done, we can get on with our Controller code. We'll load the Database library from our Model, which we will go over once the front end code is complete.

Front end code

In this section, we will go through the Controller code and create all of the view files for the front end. Once this is done, we will go through our Model. The first thing that we need to do for our Controller is to create a new file called `account.php` in the `/system/applications/controller/` directory. Once that is done, we can put the following code into it:

```
<?php
class Account extends Controller
{
  function Account()
  {
    parent::Controller();
    $this->load->library(array('form_validation', 'session'));
    $this->load->helper(array('url', 'form'));
    $this->load->model('account_model');

    $this->_salt = "123456789987654321";
  }
}
?>
```

As you can see, this is simply our class declaration and our constructor function. Take note of the resources that we are loading. We are loading two libraries: the `form_validation` library, and the `session` library. We have also loaded two helpers: the `url` and `form` helpers. Finally, we load a model called `'account_model'`—this is the model that we use to abstract our data functions out to.

I have loaded the libraries and helpers slightly differently from the previous method. You'll notice that I am passing an array of the library and helper names to the `load` function. This is because CodeIgniter can accept an array as input from the loading functions.

Here we also create a class variable for our password salt. This is important as it makes our password hashes more secure and harder to break.

Index function

The next function that we need to create is the `index` function. This is going to be fairly easy, as all we need to do is check to see if the user is logged in or not, and show them either the dashboard or the login page as appropriate. Take a look at the following code:

```
function index()
{
  if($this->account_model->logged_in() === TRUE)
  {
    $this->dashboard(TRUE);
  }
  else
  {
    $this->load->view('account/details');
  }
}
```

The first thing that we do in this function is check to see if the user is logged in, by using a function in the account model. We will build this out once the Controller is complete, so there's no need to worry about that for a while. If the function returns TRUE, the user is logged in and we load the dashboard. This is the Controller function that we will write next. If the user is not logged in, however, we show them the login page.

Details view

You'll also notice that we show a view called 'details' to a user if they go to a page which requires authentication but they are not authenticated. Create a new folder inside the /system/application/views/ directory called account—we'll use this folder to keep everything organized. Then create a file inside this directory called details.php—this is the file that we will use to show the user a friendly message asking them to either login or register an account.

```
<!DOCTYPE HTML>
<html>
<head>
<title>Login or Register to continue!</title>
</head>
<body>

<p>This page requires authorization to continue, please
  <?php echo anchor('account/login', 'Login'); ?> or
  <?php echo anchor('account/register', 'Register'); ?>
  to continue.</p>

</body>
</html>
```

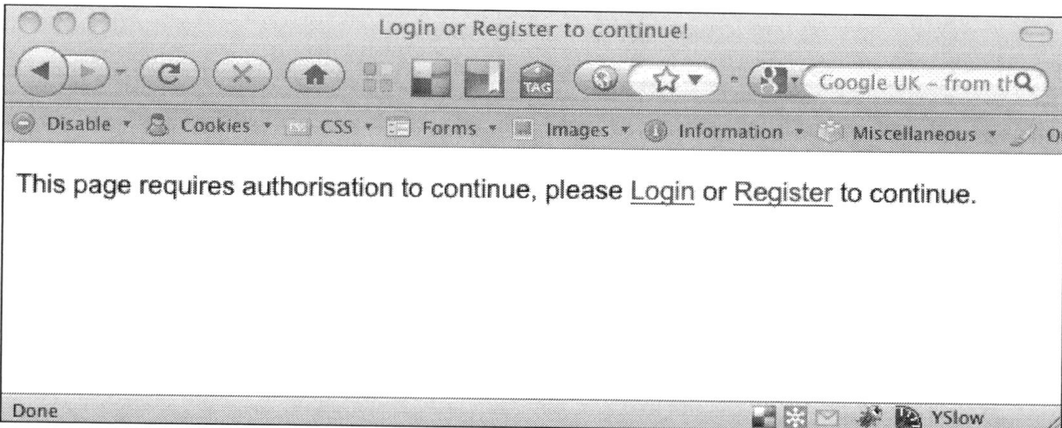

Dashboard function

This function gives us a small problem to overcome. We want to be able to call this function from other functions in the class, as we have in the `index` function. In this case we will already be checking to see if the user is logged in or not, so we may not want to perform this check twice. To overcome this, we should pass along the Boolean `TRUE` to the function, as we have already performed a check, as you can see in the previous function. Let's have a look at the dashboard function, to get a look at the function.

```
function dashboard($condition = FALSE)
{
  if($condition === TRUE
    OR $this->account_model->logged_in() === TRUE)
  {
    $this->load->view('account/dashboard');
  }
  else
  {
    $this->load->view('account/details');
  }
}
```

Let me explain this in a little more detail. If we pass the Boolean value `TRUE` to this function, then we simply load the view file. If not, and its value is `FALSE`, then we check to see if the user is logged in, and load whichever view is needed depending on whether or not they are logged in. The logic behind this is that if we have this function with no checks, then a user could go straight to it without being authenticated. But on the other hand, we don't want to check to see if someone is logged in twice. This method overcomes both problems.

Dashboard view

The dashboard view file is a simple HTML file. We display a heading tag and explain to the user what they are seeing. We also provide a logout link. Create a new file inside the `/system/application/views/account/` directory called `dashboard.php`, and paste the following code into it:

```
<!DOCTYPE HTML>
<html>
<head>
<title>Dashboard</title>
</head>
<body>
```

```
<h1>Dashboard</h1>
<p>Welcome to the Dashboard! You can only see this page when you are
logged in. This would be the page in your application where you show
users their most recent activity, anything they may have missed or
give them links to other areas of your application. In this case we
simply welcome you to the logged in area. I guess you could <?php echo
anchor('account/logout', 'logout'); ?> if you wanted to?</p>

</body>
</html>
```

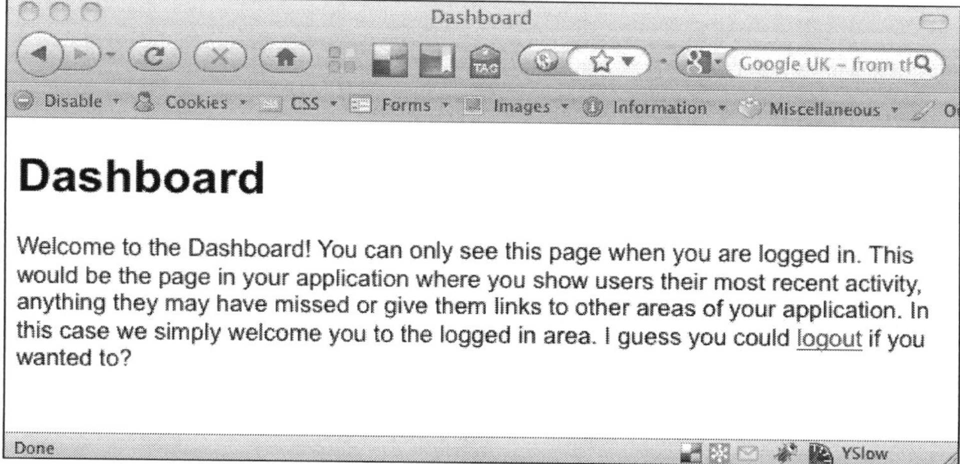

Login function

Next up, we'll build the login function. This has a lot more going on so we'll go through it one step at a time.

Form validation

The first thing that we are going to do is set some form validation rules. You'll notice that we include some callbacks in the rules. To refresh your minds, a callback is a custom function that we write to validate the content of the form field. We run everything through the XSS filter to ensure that everything we process is safe. We also set two class variables for the username and the password. This is so that we can easily access the username and password in the password check callback, as you can only send one parameter to a callback—the value of the form field.

```
function login()
{
  $this->form_validation->
```

```
        set_rules('username', 'Username',
          'xss_clean|required|callback_username_check');
      $this->form_validation->
        set_rules('password', 'Password',
          'xss_clean|required|min_length[4]|max_length[12]|sha1|
            callback_password_check');
      $this->_username = $this->input->post('username');
      $this->_password =
        sha1($this->_salt . $this->input->post('password'));
    }
```

Let's take a look at the password callback.

Password check

The password check looks for both the username and password together, to ensure the correct password was given for the username.

```
function password_check()
{
    $this->db->where('username', $this->_username);
    $query = $this->db->get('users');
    $result = $query->row_array();

    if($result['password'] == $this->_password);
    {
        return TRUE;
    }

    if($query->num_rows() == 0)
    {
        $this->form_validation->set_message('password_check',
          'There was an error!');
        return FALSE;
    }
}
```

Running the validation

The next thing that we need to do is to check if the form validation has run through its process yet. If it has, it means that the form has been submitted, and we should process the information; if not, we should show the form to the user.

```
if($this->form_validation->run() == FALSE)
{
  $this->load->view('account/login');
}
else
{
  $this->account_model->login();

  $data['message'] = "You are logged in! Now go take a look at the "
    .anchor('account/dashboard', 'Dashboard');
  $this->load->view('account/success', $data);
}
```

This code first checks to see if the form validation process has been run. If it hasn't, we show the form to the user. If it has, we log the user in by using a function in the Model, and display a success message to the user.

Full login code

Here is the full login code, for clarity.

```
function login()
{
    $this->form_validation->
      set_rules('username', 'Username',
      'xss_clean|required|callback_username_check');
    $this->form_validation->
      set_rules('password', 'Password',
      'xss_clean|required|min_length[4]|max_length[12]|sha1|
      callback_password_check');

    $this->_username = $this->input->post('username');
    $this->_password =
      sha1($this->_salt . $this->input->post('password'));

    if($this->form_validation->run() == FALSE)
    {
        $this->load->view('account/login');
    }
    else
    {
        $this->account_model->login();
```

```
            $data['message'] =
              "You are logged in! Now go take a look at the "
              . anchor('account/dashboard', 'Dashboard');
            $this->load->view('account/success', $data);
        }
    }

    function password_check()
    {
        $this->db->where('username', $this->_username);
        $query = $this->db->get('users');
        $result = $query->row_array();

        if($result['password'] == $this->_password);
        {
            return TRUE;
        }

        if($query->num_rows() == 0)
        {
            $this->form_validation->
              set_message('password_check', 'There was an error!');
            return FALSE;
        }
    }
```

Login view

Here is the code for the login view file. We're all set up to show individual errors for each field, and to repopulate the form when needed.

We also use the form helper to open the form tags, as it's easier for us to set the action of the form to a URI string.

Create a new file called `login.php` inside our `account` views sub-directory, and add the following code into it:

```
<!DOCTYPE HTML>
<html>
<head>
<title>Login</title>
</head>
<body>
```

```
<?php echo form_open('account/login'); ?>

<p>Username:</p>
<p><input type="text" name="username"
    value="<?php echo set_value('username'); ?>" /></p>
<p><?php echo form_error('username'); ?></p>

<p>Password:</p>
<p><input type="password" name="password"
    value="<?php echo set_value('password'); ?>" /></p>
<p><?php echo form_error('password'); ?></p>

<p><input type="submit" name="submit" value="Login" /></p>

</body>
</html>
```

The form will appear similar to the one shown in the next screenshot:

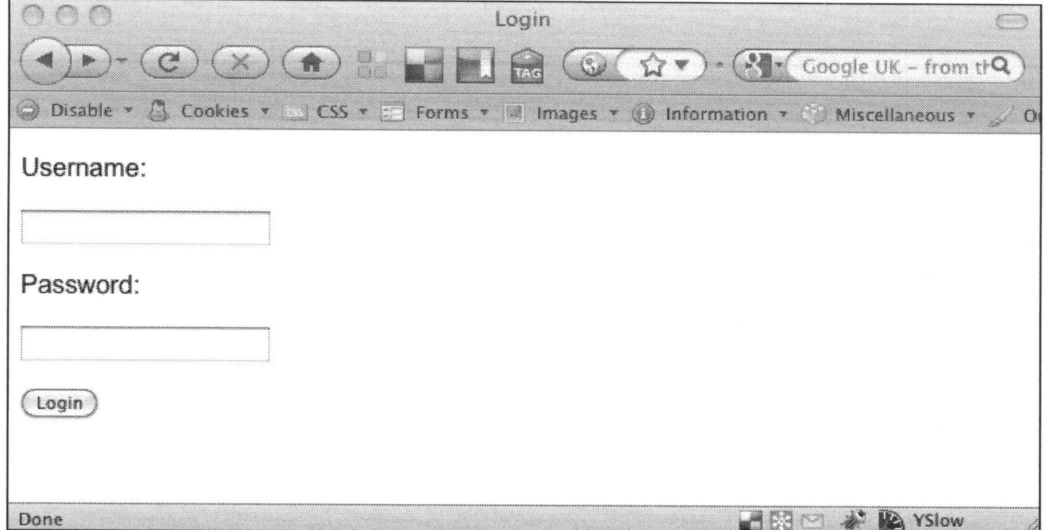

Success view

As we're using another view file for the success page, we should create it here. Create a new file inside the `account` sub-directory of `views`, called `success.php`. Put the following code into this new file:

```
<!DOCTYPE HTML>
<html>
<head>
<title>Success</title>
</head>
<body>

<h1>Success!</h1>
<p><?php echo $message; ?></p>

</body>
</html>
```

We simply echo out a variable, because each time we show this file we will have a different error message; this is the most flexible way to do this.

Register function

The `register` function works in a similar way to the `login` function. We'll split it up in the same way as we did the `login` function.

Form validation

Here is a list of the form validation rules that we set for the register form. You'll notice that we're using a callback on the user and email fields to ensure that the username and email do not already exist in the database. We also automatically `sha1` the user password fields. Once again, everything is put through the XSS filter to ensure that it's all safe.

```
function register()
{

  $this->form_validation->
    set_rules('username', 'Username', 'xss_clean|required');

  $this->form_validation->
    set_rules('email', 'Email Address',
      'xss_clean|required|valid_email|callback_email_exists');
```

```
$this->form_validation->
  set_rules('password', 'Password',
    'xss_clean|required|min_length[4]|max_length[12]|
      matches[password_conf]|sha1');

$this->form_validation->
  set_rules('password_conf', 'Password Confirmation',
    'xss_clean|required|matches[password]|sha1');
```

Take a closer look at the two password fields. You should notice one of the rules—`matches`. What this rule does is ensure that one field is exactly the same as another. We've got this function on both the password and password confirmation fields to ensure that both are exactly the same as each other.

User exists check

The callback that we use to check the username is not in use is not too dissimilar to the callbacks used in the `login` function.

```
function user_exists($user)
{
  $query = $this->db->get_where('users', array('username' => $user));

  if($query->num_rows() > 0)
  {
  $this->form_validation->set_message('user_exists', 'The
    %s already exists in our database, please use a different one.');
    return FALSE;
  }

  $query->free_result();

  return TRUE;
}
```

The function takes one parameter, which is the value of the form field. If a user types in '1234' as their username, then '1234' will be passed to this function. Then we build an SQL query to check if the username is in the database. If the query returns any number of rows (it should only return one row because of the restrictions put in place, but it's there just in case) then we set an error message to display to the user and return FALSE. This tells the Form Validation Library to stop validating the form and display the error message. If everything is fine however, we free the result and return TRUE, allowing the library to continue processing the form.

Email exists check

This function is almost identical to the previous function; the only thing that changes is that we use the word 'email' in place of 'username'. In every other case it works in an identical fashion.

```
function email_exists($email)
{
  $query = $this->db->get_where('users', array('email' => $email));

  if($query->num_rows() > 0)
  {
    $this->form_validation->set_message('email_exists',
    'The %s already exists in our database,
      please use a different one.');
    return FALSE;
  }

  $query->free_result();

  return TRUE;
}
```

Running the validation

The next thing that we need to do is to check if the validation routine is running. If it isn't running, we'll show the user the register view. If it is running, then we will take action to register the user account.

```
if($this->form_validation->run() == FALSE)
{
    $this->load->view('account/register');
}
else
{
    $data['username'] = $this->input->post('username');
    $data['email'] = $this->input->post('email');
    $data['password'] =
      sha1($this->_salt . $this->input->post('password'));

    if($this->account_model->create($data) === TRUE)
    {
        $data['message'] =
          "The user account has now been created! You can login "
          . anchor('account/login', 'here') . ".";
        $this->load->view('account/success', $data);
```

```
        }
        else
        {
          $data['error'] =
          "There was a problem when adding your account to the database.";
            $this->load->view('account/error', $data);
        }
    }
```

Let's go over adding a new user account. Once the form has been processed successfully, we set three key or value pairs in an array—`$data`. We do this by pulling in the value of the form field from the POST data by using the Input class.

Then we pass this array to a function in the model called `create`. This creates a new user account. If the function return FALSE, however, a database error has occurred and the user will be informed of that.

We then load a success or error message, depending on whether the create database operation was successful or not.

Full register code

Here is the full `register` function code, for clarity:

```
function register()
{

    $this->form_validation->
      set_rules('username', 'Username', 'xss_clean|required');
    $this->form_validation->
      set_rules('email', 'Email Address',
      'xss_clean|required|valid_email|callback_email_exists');
    $this->form_validation->
      set_rules('password', 'Password',
      'xss_clean|required|min_length[4]|max_length[12]|
      matches[password_conf]|sha1');

    $this->form_validation->
      set_rules('password_conf', 'Password Confirmation',
      'xss_clean|required|matches[password]|sha1');

    if($this->form_validation->run() == FALSE)
    {
        $this->load->view('account/register');
    }
    else
```

```
        {
            $data['username'] = $this->input->post('username');
            $data['email'] = $this->input->post('email');
            $data['password'] =
              sha1($this->_salt . $this->input->post('password'));

            if($this->account_model->create($data) === TRUE)
            {
                $data['message'] =
                "The user account has now been created! You can login "
                . anchor('account/login', 'here') . ".";
                $this->load->view('account/success', $data);
            }
            else
            {
                $data['error'] =
          "There was a problem when adding your account to the database.";
                $this->load->view('account/error', $data);
            }
        }
    }

    function user_exists($user)
    {
      $query = $this->db->
        get_where('users', array('username' => $user));

      if($query->num_rows() > 0)
      {
        $this->form_validation->set_message('user_exists', 'The
        %s already exists in our database, please use a different one.');
        return FALSE;
      }

      $query->free_result();

      return TRUE;
    }

    function email_exists($email)
    {
      $query = $this->db->get_where('users', array('email' => $email));

      if($query->num_rows() > 0)
```

```
    {
    $this->form_validation->set_message('email_exists', 'The %s
      already exists in our database, please use a different one.');
    return FALSE;
    }

    $query->free_result();

    return TRUE;
  }
```

Full controller code

Here is the full account controller code for clarity.

```
<?php

class Account extends Controller
{
 function Account()
 {
  parent::Controller();
  $this->load->library(array('form_validation', 'session'));
  $this->load->helper(array('url', 'form'));
  $this->load->model('account_model');

  $this->_salt = "123456789987654321";
 }

 function index()
 {
  if($this->account_model->logged_in() === TRUE)
  {
   $this->dashboard(TRUE);
  }
  else
  {
   $this->load->view('account/details');
  }
 }

 function dashboard($condition = FALSE)
```

```
{
 if($condition === TRUE OR $this->account_model->logged_in() === TRUE)
 {
  $this->load->view('account/dashboard');
 }
 else
 {
  $this->load->view('account/details');
 }
}

function login()
{
 $this->form_validation->
   set_rules('username', 'Username',
   'xss_clean|required|callback_username_check');
 $this->form_validation->
   set_rules('password', 'Password',
   'xss_clean|required|min_length[4]|max_length[12]|
   sha1|callback_password_check');

 $this->_username = $this->input->post('username');
 $this->_password =
   sha1($this->_salt . $this->input->post('password'));

 if($this->form_validation->run() == FALSE)
 {
  $this->load->view('account/login');
 }
 else
 {
  $this->account_model->login();

  $data['message'] =
    "You are logged in! Now go take a look at the "
    . anchor('account/dashboard', 'Dashboard');
  $this->load->view('account/success', $data);
 }
}

function register()
{

 $this->form_validation->
   set_rules('username', 'Username', 'xss_clean|required');
```

```
    $this->form_validation->
      set_rules('email', 'Email Address',
      'xss_clean|required|valid_email|callback_email_exists');
    $this->form_validation->set_rules('password', 'Password', 'xss_
clean|required|min_length[4]|max_length[12]|matches[password_
conf]|sha1');

    $this->form_validation->
      set_rules('password_conf', 'Password Confirmation',
      'xss_clean|required|matches[password]|sha1');

    if($this->form_validation->run() == FALSE)
    {
     $this->load->view('account/register');
    }
    else
    {
     $data['username'] = $this->input->post('username');
     $data['email'] = $this->input->post('email');
     $data['password'] =
       sha1($this->_salt . $this->input->post('password'));

     if($this->account_model->create($data) === TRUE)
     {
      $data['message'] =
        "The user account has now been created! You can login "
        . anchor('account/login', 'here') . ".";
      $this->load->view('account/success', $data);
     }
     else
     {
      $data['error'] =
        "There was a problem when adding your account to the database.";
      $this->load->view('account/error', $data);
     }
    }
  }

  function logout()
  {
   $this->session->sess_destroy();
   $this->load->view('account/logout');
  }

  function password_check()
  {
```

```
      $this->db->where('username', $this->_username);
      $query = $this->db->get('users');
      $result = $query->row_array();
      if($result['password'] == $this->_password);
      {
       return TRUE;
      }

      if($query->num_rows() == 0)
      {
       $this->form_validation->
         set_message('password_check', 'There was an error!');
       return FALSE;
      }
     }

     function user_exists($user)
     {
      $query = $this->db->get_where('users', array('username' => $user));

      if($query->num_rows() > 0)
      {
       $this->form_validation->
         set_message('user_exists',
    'The %s already exists in our database, please use a different one.');
       return FALSE;
      }

      $query->free_result();

      return TRUE;
     }

     function email_exists($email)
     {
      $query = $this->db->get_where('users', array('email' => $email));

      if($query->num_rows() > 0)
      {
       $this->form_validation->
         set_message('email_exists',
    'The %s already exists in our database, please use a different one.');
       return FALSE;
      }

      $query->free_result();
```

```
    return TRUE;
  }


}

?>
```

Register view

Now we need to create our view file. Create a new file in the `account` directory called `register.php`, and insert the following code into this new file:

```
<!DOCTYPE HTML>
<html>
<head>
<title>Register</title>
</head>
<body>

<?php echo form_open('account/register'); ?>

<p>Username:</p>
<p><input type="text" name="username"
  value="<?php echo set_value('username'); ?>" /></p>
<p><?php echo form_error('username'); ?></p>

<p>Email:</p>
<p><input type="text" name="email"
    value="<?php echo set_value('email'); ?>" /></p>
<p><?php echo form_error('email'); ?></p>

<p>Password:</p>
<p><input type="password" name="password"
    value="<?php echo set_value('password'); ?>" /></p>
<p><?php echo form_error('password'); ?></p>

<p>Password Confirmation:</p>
<p><input type="password" name="password_conf"
    value="<?php echo set_value('password_conf'); ?>" /></p>
<p><?php echo form_error('password_conf'); ?></p>
<p><input type="submit" name="submit"
    value="Register Account" /></p>

</body>
</html>
```

The registration form should appear similar to the one shown in following screenshot:

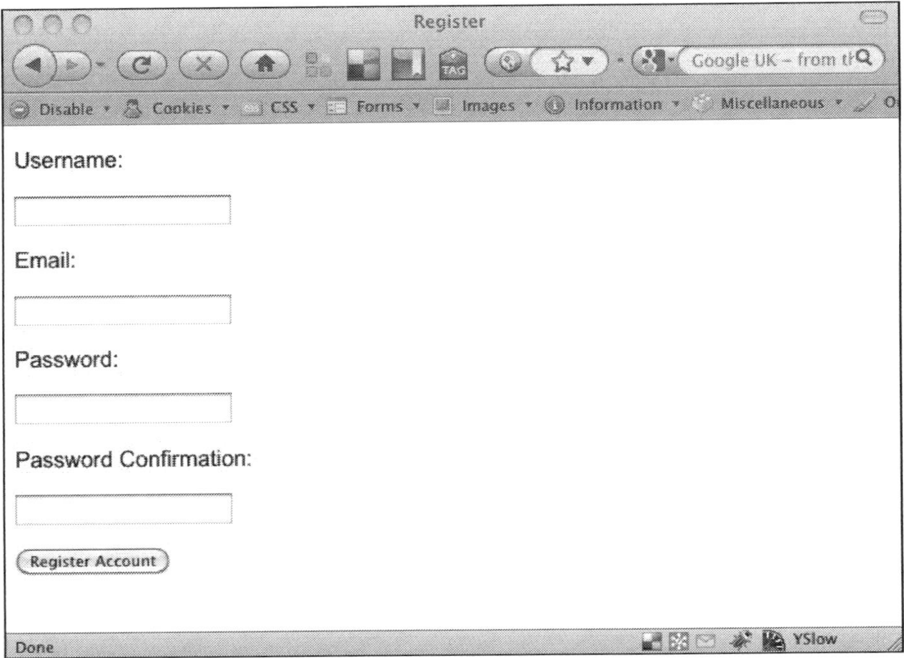

You should be able to see some similarities between this view and that of the login form. There's just more fields to deal with.

Error view

We didn't need a view file for any errors for the `login` function, but we do for the `register` function. In any scenario, it's unlikely that anyone will see this error, because if the application isn't connected to the database a CodeIgniter error will be displayed. However, we will cover all eventualities. Create a new file inside our `account` view directory called `error.php`. This is what the file's content looks like:

```
<!DOCTYPE HTML>
<html>
<head>
  <title>Error</title>
</head>
<body>

<h1>Error</h1>
```

```
<p><?php echo $error; ?></p>

</body>
</html>
```

Logout function

As well as registering and logging in, we also want to allow our users to log out. Here's how we do that:

```
function logout()
{
  $this->session->sess_destroy();
  $this->load->view('account/logout');
}
```

This function is pretty simple. We destroy any session data that has been saved in the CodeIgniter Session library—this is the part that logs the user out. The next line simply loads in the logout view.

Logout view

Create a new file—again inside our `account` view directory—called `logout.php`, and put the following code into it:

```
<!DOCTYPE HTML>
<html>
<head>
<title>Logout</title>
</head>
<body>

<h1>Success!</h1>
<p>You are now logged out! You can log back in again
  <?php echo anchor('account/login', 'here'); ?>.</p>

</body>
</html>
```

The logout screen should appear similar to the one shown in the next screenshot:

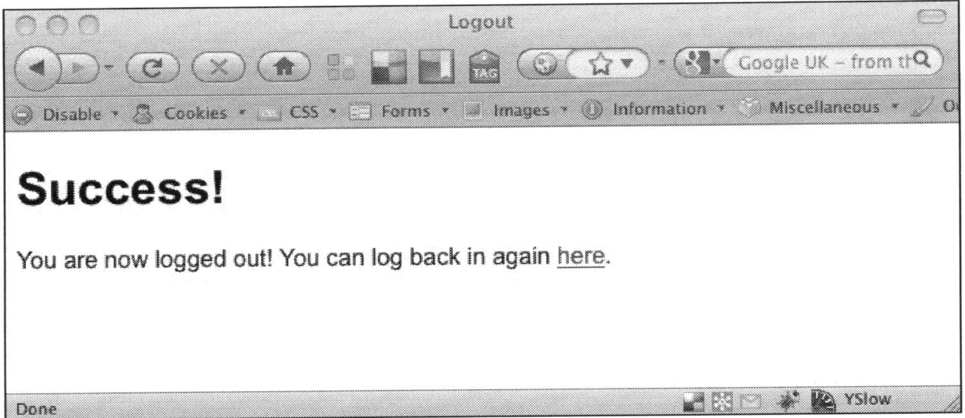

Model code

The Model is a very important piece of the puzzle. If you tried to register a user account you will see an error message, because currently the Model does not exist. Let's add it now. Create a new file inside the `/system/application/models/` directory, and call it `account_model.php`.

Model constructor

Here's what our Model constructor looks like. It's very simple, as we're simply calling on the parent class construct and loading the database library.

```
<?php
class Account_model extends Model
{
  function Account_model()
  {
    parent::Model();
    $this->load->database();
  }
}
?>
```

Create function

The `create` function is as simple as it could get, thanks to CodeIgniter's Active Record implementation. We can simple take the array passed to it and insert it into the database by using the `insert()` function.

```
function create($data)
{
  if($this->db->insert('users', $data))
  {
    return TRUE;
  }

  return FALSE;
}
```

We always return either TRUE or FALSE in capital letters, as this is what is set out in the CodeIgniter PHP Style Guide. We don't have to conform to the Style Guide, but it helps.

Login function

The `login` function creates a new session for the user, and adds the username and the Boolean `logged_in`, set to `TRUE`. Once again, this is made incredibly easy by the CodeIgniter Session library.

```
function login()
{
  $data = array(
          'username' => $this->input->post('username'),
          'logged_in' => TRUE
          );

  $this->session->set_userdata($data);
}
```

Logged in check function

This function checks the `session` data of a user to see whether or not they are logged in. If they are we return TRUE and if not we return FALSE.

```
function logged_in()
{
  if($this->session->userdata('logged_in') == TRUE)
  {
```

```
      return TRUE;
    }

    return FALSE;
  }
```

Full model code

Once again, here is the full Model code, for clarity:

```
<?php

class Account_model extends Model
{
  function Account_model()
  {
    parent::Model();
    $this->load->database();
  }

  function create($data)
  {
    if($this->db->insert('users', $data))
    {
      return TRUE;
    }

    return FALSE;

  }

  function login()
  {
    $data = array(
              'username' => $this->input->post('username'),
              'logged_in' => TRUE
    );
    $this->session->set_userdata($data);
  }

  function logged_in()
  {
    if($this->session->userdata('logged_in') == TRUE)
    {
```

```
            return TRUE;
        }

    return FALSE;
    }
}
?>
```

Addressing some issues

Firstly, it's easier to teach you the principle behind user authentication and the MVC design pattern as a whole. Hopefully you can see that a Model is not simply a database abstraction layer, but a data abstraction layer. In the Account Model, we use it to handle both database interaction and session manipulation.

Secondly, as we were using the Form Validation Library and were using callbacks, we needed to use a Controller. The Form Validation Library only allows callbacks to be inside a Controller. If I had used a Library, I would have needed to use an extended Controller, and that's too complicated for users inexperienced with the framework.

Finally, the way that we've built it is the way that many people do it anyway. I have already created my own authentication library, aptly named **The Authentication Library**, which people can use. This way, however, is more suited to the MVC style for newer users. Everything is laid out in an easy way and it is much easier to pick up the principle of user authentication.

I'm hoping that by learning the principle behind things, and not just directly copying from the book, that you will be able to code these things much more quickly; and you'll know which way is the best when you need to do things for yourself.

The Authentication Library

If you are looking for a third-party authentication library with a lot more features than the one we are able to build in a chapter in a book, may I recommend my own library—"**The Authentication Library**"—as an alternative.

The Authentication Library includes a secure 'remember me' function, which allows users to stay logged in without the possibility of their cookies being stolen or forged by malicious users to gain unauthorized access to your systems.

The best part of The Authentication Library is that all you need to do to use it is to extend a different Controller. Rather than extending the default `Controller` class, you would instead extend the `Application` class. You don't need to build any forms or process the forms—it is all taken care of for you. It is the easiest method of authentication for CodeIgniter, as you don't really need to do anything.

To find out more about The Authentication Library, you can read the User Guide I've written for it, at `http://www.adamgriffiths.co.uk/user_guide/` or alternatively go straight to the download over on Github at `http://github.com/adamgriffiths/the-codeigniter-authentication-library/tree/master/`.

Summary

There we have it. An easy way to authenticate users, without relying on a third-party system. We used a Controller and Model instead of a Library, and we used the Model to access two types of data sources—a database and a session.

In the next chapter, we'll create a new set of libraries that will allow us to authenticate users by using Twitter oAuth and Facebook Connect.

5
User Authentication 2

User authentication is an important part of many applications. Now that we've built our own authentication method, let's look at how we would utilize third-party authentication methods.

In this chapter we will:

- Learn how Twitter oAuth and Facebook Connect work
- Create a library for each authentication method
- Utilize these libraries in order to create separate applications to demonstrate how each works, and the differences between the two protocols

Using Twitter oAuth

oAuth is an open protocol for secure user authentication across APIs. It allows users to gain limited access to websites by using their Twitter credentials. It's a very sound method of user authentication, and doesn't take too much work to get going. Twitter oAuth is used by hundreds of third-party Twitter clients and mashups—just to give you an idea of how useful it can be.

How oAuth works

Getting used to how Twitter oAuth works takes a little time.

When a user comes to your login page, you send a `GET` request to Twitter for a set of request codes. These request codes are used to verify the user on the Twitter website.

The user then goes through to Twitter to either allow or deny your application access to their account. If they allow the application access, they will be taken back to your application. The URL they get sent to will have an oAuth token appended to the end. This is used in the next step.

Back at your application, you then send another `GET` request for some access codes from Twitter. These access codes are used to verify that the user has come directly from Twitter, and has not tried to spoof an oAuth token in their web browser.

Registering a Twitter application

Before we write any code, we need to register an application with Twitter. This will give us the two access codes that we need. The first is a consumer key, and the second is a secret key. Both are used to identify our application, so if someone posts a message to Twitter through our application, our application name will show up alongside the user's tweet.

To register a new application with Twitter, you need to go to `http://www.twitter.com/apps/new`. You'll be asked for a photo for your application and other information, such as website URL, callback URL, and a description, among other things.

You must select the checkbox that reads **Yes, use Twitter for login** or you will not be able to authenticate any accounts with your application keys.

Once you've filled out the form, you'll be able to see your consumer key and consumer secret code. You'll need these later. Don't worry though; you'll be able to get to these at any time so there's no need to save them to your hard drive. Here's a screenshot of my application:

Downloading the oAuth library

Before we get to write any of our CodeIgniter wrapper library, we need to download the oAuth PHP library. This allows us to use the oAuth protocol without writing the code from scratch ourselves.

You can find the PHP Library on the oAuth website at `www.oauth.net/code`. Scroll down to PHP and click on the link to download the **basic PHP Library**; or just visit: `http://oauth.googlecode.com/svn/code/php/`—the file you need is named `OAuth.php`.

Download this file and save it in the folder `system/application/libraries/twitter/`—you'll need to create the `twitter` folder. We're simply going to create a folder for each different protocol so that we can easily distinguish between them.

Once you've done that, we'll create our Library file. Create a new file in the `system/application/libraries/` folder, called `Twitter_oauth.php`. This is the file that will contain functions to obtain both request and access tokens from Twitter, and verify the user credentials.

The next section of the chapter will go through the process of creating this library alongside the Controller implementation; this is because the whole process requires work on both the front-end and the back-end. Bear with me, as it could get a little confusing, especially when trying to implement a brand new type of system such as Twitter oAuth.

Library base class

Let's break things down into small sections. The following code is a version of the base class with all its guts pulled out. It simply loads the oAuth library and sets up a set of variables for us to store certain information in. Below this, I'll go over what each of the variables are there for.

```
<?php

require_once(APPPATH . 'libraries/twitter/OAuth.php');

class Twitter_oauth
{

  var $consumer;
  var $token;
  var $method;
  var $http_status;
  var $last_api_call;

}
?>
```

The first variable you'll see is `$consumer`—it is used to store the credentials for our application keys and the user tokens as and when we get them.

The second variable you see on the list is `$token`—this is used to store the user credentials. A new instance of the oAuth class `OAuthConsumer` is created and stored in this variable.

Thirdly, you'll see the variable `$method`—this is used to store the oAuth Signature Method (the way we sign our oAuth calls).

Finally, the last two variables, `$http_status` and `$last_api_call`, are used to store the last HTTP Status Code and the URL of the last API call, respectively. These two variables are used solely for debugging purposes.

Controller base class

The Controller is the main area where we'll be working, so it is crucial that we design the best way to use it so that we don't have to repeat our code. Therefore, we're going to have our consumer key and consumer secret key in the Controller. Take a look at the Base of our class to get a better idea of what I mean.

```
<?php
session_start();

class Twitter extends Controller
{

  var $data;

  function Twitter()
  {
    parent::Controller();

    $this->data['consumer_key'] = "";
    $this->data['consumer_secret'] = "";
}
```

The global variable `$data` will be used to store our consumer key and consumer secret. These must not be left empty and will be provided to you by Twitter when creating your application. We use these when instantiating the Library class, which is why we need it available throughout the Controller instead of just in one function.

We also allow for sessions to be used in the Controller, as we want to temporarily store some of the data that we get from Twitter in a session. We could use the CodeIgniter Session Library, but it doesn't offer us as much flexibility as native PHP sessions; this is because with native sessions we don't need to rely on cookies and a database, so we'll stick with the native sessions for this Controller.

Library constructor

The Library constructor needs to know if we have an authenticated user or not. So here's what we do. Firstly, we set up a new instance of the oAuth Consumer class, creating our application details. Then we check to see if oAuth tokens have been passed to the function. If they have, it means that the user has returned from Twitter; if not, they have just come onto the site and are ready to click on the link to authenticate themselves. We pass the data to the function as an array, as this is the only way that CodeIgniter lets us do this with the `$this->load->library` function.

```
function Twitter_oauth($data)
{
  $this->method = new OAuthSignatureMethod_HMAC_SHA1();
  $this->consumer = new OAuthConsumer($data['consumer_key'],
      $data['consumer_secret']);

  if(!empty($data['oauth_token'])
    && !empty($data['oauth_token_secret']))
  {
    $this->token = new OAuthConsumer($data['oauth_token'],
      $data['oauth_token_secret']);
  }
  else
  {
    $this->token = NULL;
  }
}
```

Requesting user tokens

The first thing that we need to do to authenticate a user is to query Twitter for request tokens. These tokens are used to authenticate a user to let Twitter know that they came from our application. Let's take a look at the function for requesting tokens:

```
function get_request_token()
{
  $args = array();

  $request = OAuthRequest::
```

```
    from_consumer_and_token($this->consumer, $this->token,
      'GET', "https://twitter.com/oauth/request_token", $args);
  $request->sign_request($this->method, $this->consumer, $this->token);
  $request = $this->http($request->to_url());

  $token = $this->parse_request($request);

  $this->token = new OAuthConsumer($token['oauth_token'],
  $token['oauth_token_secret']);

  return $token;
  }
```

As you can see here, we are using the OAuthRequest class provided by us in the PHP library that we downloaded earlier, to set up a new request to Twitter. Next, we have to sign our request; this is so that we can encrypt data between our own application and Twitter. The final thing that we do to complete the request is to use a function called `http()` to go ahead and pull the data from Twitter.

Once this is all done, we pass the array to the function `parse_request()` — this simply parses all of the data for this request, and gives it back to us in an associative array.

Finally, after all of that is complete, we can create a new instance of the `OAuthConsumer` class, with the new tokens from Twitter. Then we simply return the tokens from the function in a variable.

HTTP function

Because this is quite a large dependant to the previous function, we'll go through building it here. This function is slightly more complex than the others. We use cURL to initiate the request to Twitter and to return all values from Twitter. If you already have some cURL knowledge, then you can skip the explanation after the next code block.

```
function http($url, $post_data = null)
{
  $ch = curl_init();

  if(defined("CURL_CA_BUNDLE_PATH"))
    curl_setopt($ch, CURLOPT_CAINFO, CURL_CA_BUNDLE_PATH);

  curl_setopt($ch, CURLOPT_URL, $url);
  curl_setopt($ch, CURLOPT_CONNECTTIMEOUT, 30);
  curl_setopt($ch, CURLOPT_TIMEOUT, 30);
```

```
    curl_setopt($ch, CURLOPT_RETURNTRANSFER, 1);
    curl_setopt($ch, CURLOPT_SSL_VERIFYPEER, 0);

    if(isset($post_data))
    {
      curl_setopt($ch, CURLOPT_POST, 1);
      curl_setopt($ch, CURLOPT_POSTFIELDS, $post_data);
    }

    $response = curl_exec($ch);
    $this->http_status = curl_getinfo($ch, CURLINFO_HTTP_CODE);
    $this->last_api_call = $url;
    curl_close($ch);

    return $response;
}
```

The first thing that we need to do to use cURL is run the `curl_init()` function. This will return a cURL handle to a function. All subsequent functions must pass this handle as their first parameter.

Observe the following code:

```
if(defined("CURL_CA_BUNDLE_PATH"))
    curl_setopt($ch, CURLOPT_CAINFO, CURL_CA_BUNDLE_PATH);
```

This allows us to validate the SSL certificate to make sure that the peer's SSL certificate is valid. In short we setup cURL to check if Twitter's SSL certificate is valid.

The next few lines of code set up the connection to the URL and set some conditions for the connection, such as the timeout, and set the SSL verifier to false.

Next up, we check to see if the variable `$post_data` has already been set. This will set the data that we would like to send to Twitter if we make a POST request. This is setting up the Library so we can send status messages to Twitter if we wanted to.

Finally, we get to the part of the code that performs the operation:

```
$response = curl_exec($ch);
$this->http_status = curl_getinfo($ch, CURLINFO_HTTP_CODE);
$this->last_api_call = $url;
curl_close($ch);
```

The first line shown here executes our cURL session. This will return the result on success, or FALSE upon failure. The next two lines simply save some details for debugging purposes, and then on the last line we close the cURL session.

The very last line of this function returns the **$response** variable, which contains the data from the request.

Parse function

The next dependant function we have is the one that parses the response from Twitter into an array that we can actually use.

Observe the following function:

```
function parse_request($string)
{
  $args = explode("&", $string);
  $args[] = explode("=", $args['0']);
  $args[] = explode("=", $args['1']);

  $token[$args['2']['0']] = $args['2']['1'];
  $token[$args['3']['0']] = $args['3']['1'];

  return $token;
}
```

This function takes a string and splits it up at every occurrence of an ampersand (&). This splits it up into an array with two key value pairs. Then we split those two pairs at the equals (=) sign. Then we simply format them so that instead of the array keys being numbers, they are `oauth_token` and `oauth_token_secret`—the two items that we parse in the function.

Controller index function

As all Controllers have a default function called `index`, this is where we will start our code. The `index` function will get request tokens from Twitter and then build a URL from that. The URL will go to Twitter with one of the tokens attached, so that Twitter knows the user has come from our application. We'll save these tokens in a session so that we can verify the user when they come back to our application from Twitter.

```
function index()
{
  $this->load->library('twitter_oauth', $this->data);

  $token = $this->twitter_oauth->get_request_token();
```

```
    $_SESSION['oauth_request_token'] = $token['oauth_token'];
    $_SESSION['oauth_request_token_secret'] =
      $token['oauth_token_secret'];

    $request_link = $this->twitter_oauth->get_authorize_URL($token);

    $data['link'] = $request_link;
    $this->load->view('twitter/home', $data);
}
```

As you can see here, the first thing that we do is load the Twitter oAuth library and pass the global variables to it—our consumer key and consumer secret. The next thing that we do is get the request tokens from Twitter and then save these to a session. The next line is where we build the request link, so that when we link people to Twitter they'll be recognized correctly. This uses a function `get_authorize_url()`, which we'll build in the next section. Then we put this link into an array so that we can easily pass it to the view file.

get_authorize_URL function

This function takes the token passed to it and appends it to a Twitter URL. It's fairly straightforward.

```
function get_authorize_URL($token)
{
  if(is_array($token)) $token = $token['oauth_token'];
  return "https://twitter.com/oauth/authorize?oauth_token=" . $token;
}
```

Main view file

We need to create a folder for our Twitter-related view files. Go ahead and create a folder inside the `system/application/views/` folder, called `twitter`. This is simply to make everything easily maintainable. When that's done, create a new file called `home.php` and, enter the code given next.

This is a simple HTML page that just echoes out the URL to Twitter so that users can easily be authorized. You'll notice the only element on the page is the link to Twitter. Right now we don't need to include anything else.

```
<!DOCTYPE HTML>
<html>
<head>
<title>Twitter oAuth</title>
</head>
```

```
<body>

<p>
  <a href="<?php echo $link; ?>">
    Click here to login with Twitter oAuth</a>
</p>

</body>
</html>
```

This is simply a link. In a browser, it should appear similar to the example shown in the next screenshot:

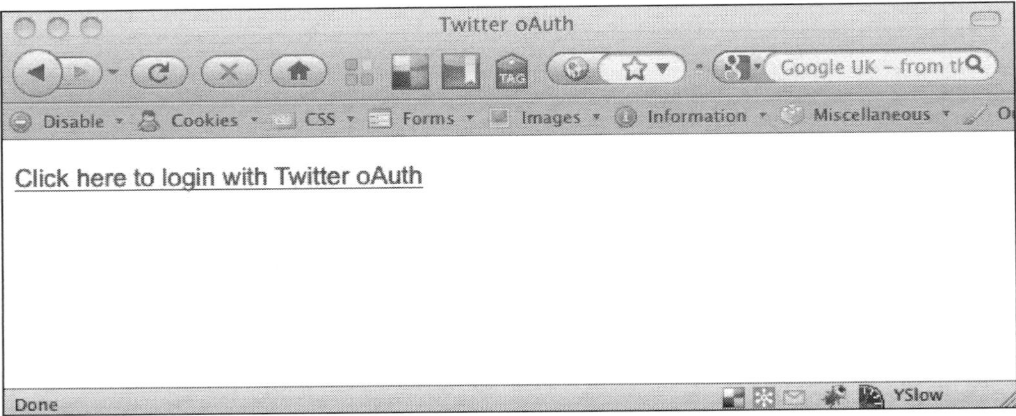

Change your callback URL

Once a user comes back to your application, you can verify their new access tokens with Twitter to ensure that they have come from Twitter and are not trying to spoof tokens to gain unauthorized access to your application. For this, we need to change our callback URL slightly.

We'll be creating a function in our Twitter Controller that will handle all of this; it will be called **access()**—this is where you need to change your callback URL. It should look something like this:

```
http://www.example.com/index.php/twitter/access/
```

That way, when a user comes back to your application, they will be in the right place for you do to the rest of the legwork.

Creating the access function

The access function does a few things that are crucial to authenticating users correctly. Firstly, we set the tokens that we saved in the sessions and pass them to the library in order to create a new instance of the oAuth Consumer class, but this time as the user who is using the users tokens. Next, we query Twitter for access tokens. These are the tokens that verify that the user has come from Twitter and that we can authenticate them. Once that is done, we save the new tokens and then display another view file. The view file simply tells you to take a look at your connections page on Twitter to check if your application is on there.

```
function access()
{
  $this->data['oauth_token'] = $_SESSION['oauth_request_token'];
  $this->data['oauth_token_secret'] =
    $_SESSION['oauth_request_token_secret'];

  $this->load->library('twitter_oauth', $this->data);

  $tokens = $this->twitter_oauth->get_access_token();

  $_SESSION['oauth_access_token'] = $tokens['oauth_token'];
  $_SESSION['oauth_access_token_secret'] =
    $tokens['oauth_token_secret'];

  $this->load->view('twitter/accessed', $tokens);
}
```

The view file

The view file that we use for this is very simple. We passed the `$tokens` variable to the view file; this lets us echo the user's screen name in the title of the page.

```
<!DOCTYPE HTML>
<html>
<head>
<title>Twitter oAuth - @<?php echo $screen_name; ?></title>
</head>
<body>

<p>Your account should now be registered with Twitter. Check here:
  <a href="https://twitter.com/account/connections">
    https://twitter.com/account/connections
  </a>
</p>

</body>
</html>
```

The page should appear similar to the example shown in the next screenshot:

Getting access tokens

Getting the access tokens from Twitter takes two new functions. Firstly, there is the function `get_access_tokens()`, which is almost identical to the `get_request_tokens()` function. Then there is a new function called `parse_access()` – this is very much like the `parse_request()` function, although it works slightly differently.

get_access_tokens()

This function works in almost exactly the same way as the `get_request_tokens()` function. It just queries a different URL and uses a different parsing function.

```
function get_access_token()
{
  $args = array();

  $request = OAuthRequest::
    from_consumer_and_token($this->consumer, $this->token, 'GET',
      "https://twitter.com/oauth/access_token", $args);
  $request->
    sign_request($this->method, $this->consumer, $this->token);
  $request = $this->http($request->to_url());

  $token = $this->parse_access($request);

  $this->token = new OAuthConsumer($token['oauth_token'],
    $token['oauth_token_secret']);

    return $token;
}
```

parse_access()

This function takes the string returned from Twitter and splits it up at each `&` and `=`, splitting them into pairs of array keys and values. The function then returns the array for use in the class.

```
function parse_access($string)
{
  $r = array();

  foreach(explode('&', $string) as $param)
  {
    $pair = explode('=', $param, 2);
    if(count($pair) != 2) continue;
    $r[urldecode($pair[0])] = urldecode($pair[1]);
  }

  return $r;
}
```

Logging out

When you log users out of your application, you need to destroy all session data. This is so that you can easily create a new session for them if they wish to log in again with a clean slate. Here's the function to do this.

This should go in your Controller code so that you can access it from the URI `index.php/twitter/logout/`.

```
function logout()
{
  session_destroy();

  $this->load->view('twitter/logout');
}
```

The view file for this page is fairly simple. Create a new file inside your Twitter `views` folder called `logout.php`.

```
<!DOCTYPE HTML>
<html>
<head>
<title>Twitter oAuth - Logged Out</title>
</head>
<body>
```

```
<p>You are no longer logged in!</p>

</body>
</html>
```

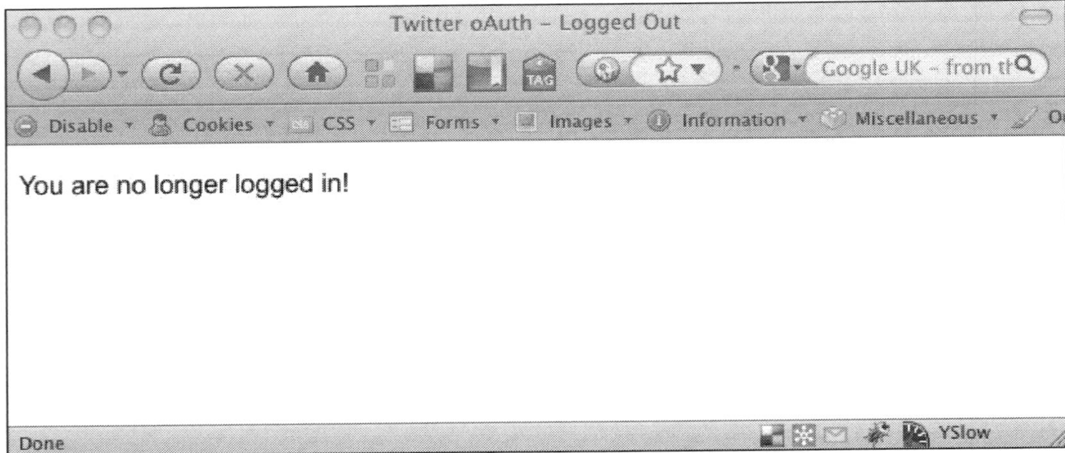

Debug function

We should add in a debug function for ease of use. When the debug function is called, we want to echo out the URL of the last API call, and the HTTP Status Code. Here's how we do that:

```
function debug_info()
{
  echo("Last API Call: ".$this->last_api_call."<br />\n");
  echo("Response Code: ".$this->http_status."<br />\n");
}
```

Final library code

Here is the final library code, in context:

```
<?php

require_once(APPPATH . 'libraries/twitter/OAuth.php');

class Twitter_oauth
{

  var $consumer;
```

```
var $token;
var $method;
var $http_status;
var $last_api_call;

function Twitter_oauth($data)
{
  $this->method = new OAuthSignatureMethod_HMAC_SHA1();
  $this->consumer = new OAuthConsumer($data['consumer_key'],
    $data['consumer_secret']);

  if(!empty($data['oauth_token'])
    && !empty($data['oauth_token_secret']))
  {
    $this->token = new OAuthConsumer($data['oauth_token'],
      $data['oauth_token_secret']);
  }
  else
  {
    $this->token = NULL;
  }
}

function debug_info()
{
  echo("Last API Call: ".$this->last_api_call."<br />\n");
  echo("Response Code: ".$this->http_status."<br />\n");
}

function get_request_token()
{
  $args = array();

  $request = OAuthRequest::from_consumer_and_token($this->consumer,
    $this->token, 'GET',
      "https://twitter.com/oauth/request_token", $args);
  $request->sign_request($this->method, $this->consumer,
    $this->token);
  $request = $this->http($request->to_url());

  $token = $this->parse_request($request);

  $this->token = new OAuthConsumer($token['oauth_token'],
    $token['oauth_token_secret']);
```

```
        return $token;
    }

    function get_access_token()
    {
      $args = array();

      $request = OAuthRequest::from_consumer_and_token($this->consumer,
        $this->token, 'GET', "https://twitter.com/oauth/access_token",
          $args);
      $request->sign_request($this->method, $this->consumer,
        $this->token);
      $request = $this->http($request->to_url());

      $token = $this->parse_access($request);

      $this->token = new OAuthConsumer($token['oauth_token'],
        $token['oauth_token_secret']);

      return $token;
    }

    function parse_request($string)
    {
      $args = explode("&", $string);
      $args[] = explode("=", $args['0']);
      $args[] = explode("=", $args['1']);

      $token[$args['2']['0']] = $args['2']['1'];
      $token[$args['3']['0']] = $args['3']['1'];

      return $token;
    }

    function parse_access($string)
    {
      $r = array();

      foreach(explode('&', $string) as $param)
      {
        $pair = explode('=', $param, 2);
        if(count($pair) != 2) continue;
        $r[urldecode($pair[0])] = urldecode($pair[1]);
      }
```

```
    return $r;
  }

  function get_authorize_URL($token)
  {
    if(is_array($token)) $token = $token['oauth_token'];
    return "https://twitter.com/oauth/authorize?oauth_token=" .
      $token;
  }

  function http($url, $post_data = null)
  {
    $ch = curl_init();

    if(defined("CURL_CA_BUNDLE_PATH"))
      curl_setopt($ch, CURLOPT_CAINFO, CURL_CA_BUNDLE_PATH);

    curl_setopt($ch, CURLOPT_URL, $url);
    curl_setopt($ch, CURLOPT_CONNECTTIMEOUT, 30);
    curl_setopt($ch, CURLOPT_TIMEOUT, 30);
    curl_setopt($ch, CURLOPT_RETURNTRANSFER, 1);
    curl_setopt($ch, CURLOPT_SSL_VERIFYPEER, 0);

    if(isset($post_data))
    {
      curl_setopt($ch, CURLOPT_POST, 1);
      curl_setopt($ch, CURLOPT_POSTFIELDS, $post_data);
    }

    $response = curl_exec($ch);
    $this->http_status = curl_getinfo($ch, CURLINFO_HTTP_CODE);
    $this->last_api_call = $url;
    curl_close($ch);

    return $response;
  }

}

?>
```

Final controller code

Here is the final Controller code, in context:

```
<?php
session_start();

class Twitter extends Controller
{

  var $data;

  function Twitter()
  {
    parent::Controller();

    $this->data['consumer_key'] = "";
    $this->data['consumer_secret'] = "";
  }

  function index()
  {
    $this->load->library('twitter_oauth', $this->data);

    $token = $this->twitter_oauth->get_request_token();

    $_SESSION['oauth_request_token'] = $token['oauth_token'];
    $_SESSION['oauth_request_token_secret'] =
      $token['oauth_token_secret'];

    $request_link = $this->twitter_oauth->get_authorize_URL($token);

    $data['link'] = $request_link;
    $this->load->view('twitter/home', $data);
  }

  function access()
  {
    $this->data['oauth_token'] = $_SESSION['oauth_request_token'];
    $this->data['oauth_token_secret'] =
      $_SESSION['oauth_request_token_secret'];
```

```
        $this->load->library('twitter_oauth', $this->data);

        /* Request access tokens from twitter */
        $tokens = $this->twitter_oauth->get_access_token();

        /*Save the access tokens.*/
        /*Normally these would be saved in a database for future use. */
        $_SESSION['oauth_access_token'] = $tokens['oauth_token'];
        $_SESSION['oauth_access_token_secret'] =
          $tokens['oauth_token_secret'];


        $this->load->view('twitter/accessed', $tokens);
    }

    function logout()
    {
        session_destroy();
        $this->load->view('twitter/logout');
    }
}

?>
```

Using Facebook Connect

Facebook Connect is just like Twitter oAuth, but for Facebook accounts. It doesn't use the oAuth protocol, so its workings might seem slightly different to developers. To users, however, the difference is marginal.

Just like in Twitter oAuth, users do not need to enter any of their account credentials on your website or application—it is all handled by Facebook.

Registering a Facebook application

You need to register a new Facebook Application so that you can get an API key and an Application Secret Key. Head on over to `www.facebook.com/developers/` and click on the **Set up New Application** button in the upper right-hand corner.

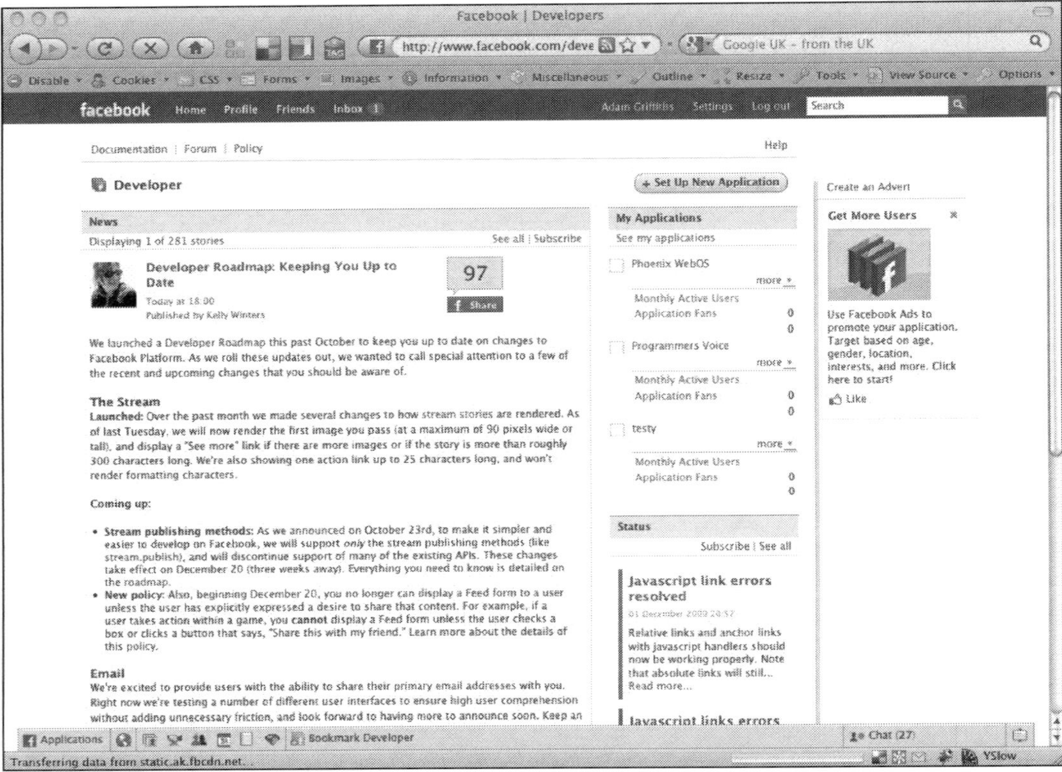

This process is very similar to setting up a new Twitter application, so I won't bore you with all of the details.

Once you've done that, you should have your API key and Application Secret Key. These two things will enable Facebook to recognize your application.

Download the Client library

When you are on your applications page showing all your applications' information, scroll down the page to see a link to download the Client Library. Once you've downloaded it, simply untar it.

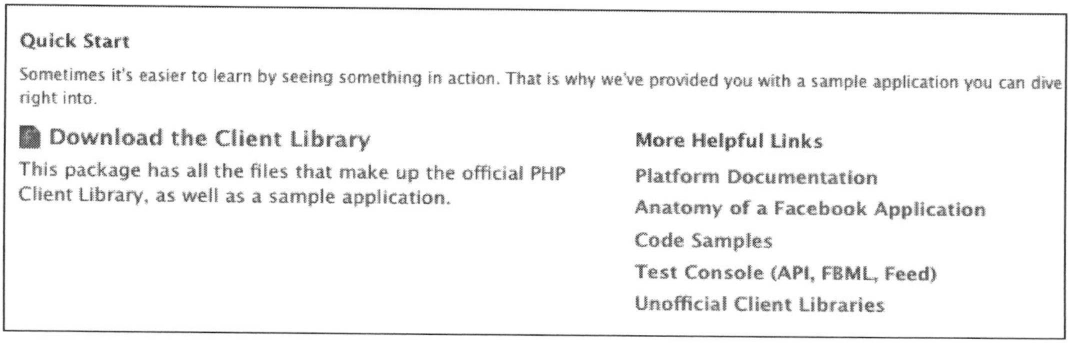

Quick Start

Sometimes it's easier to learn by seeing something in action. That is why we've provided you with a sample application you can dive right into.

Download the Client Library

This package has all the files that make up the official PHP Client Library, as well as a sample application.

More Helpful Links

Platform Documentation

Anatomy of a Facebook Application

Code Samples

Test Console (API, FBML, Feed)

Unofficial Client Libraries

There are two folders inside the `facebook-platform` folder, `footprints` and `php`. We are only going to be using the `php` folder. Open up the `php` folder; there are two files here that we don't need, `facebook_desktop.php` and `facebook_mobile.php`—you can delete them.

Finally, we can copy this folder into our application. Place it in the `system/application/libraries` folder, and then rename the folder to `facebook`. This helps us to keep our code tidy and properly sorted.

Our CodeIgniter Wrapper

Before we start coding, we need to know what we need to code in order to make the Facebook Client Library work with our CodeIgniter installation.

Our Wrapper library needs to instantiate the Facebook class with our API Key and Secret Application Key. We'll also want it to create a session for the user when they are logged in. If a session is found but the user is not authenticated, we will need to destroy the session.

You should create a new file in the `system/application/libraries/` folder, called `Facebook_connect.php`. This is where the Library code given next should be placed.

Base class

The Base Class for our Facebook Connect Wrapper Library is very simple:

```
<?php

require_once(APPPATH . 'libraries/facebook/facebook.php');

class Facebook_connect
{
  var $CI;
  var $connection;

  var $api_key;
  var $secret_key;
  var $user;
  var $user_id;
  var $client;
}

?>
```

The first thing that our Library needs to do is to load the Facebook library—the one we downloaded from `facebook.com`. We build the path for this by using **APPPATH**, a constant defined by CodeIgniter to be the path of the application folder.

Then, in our Class we have a set of variables. The `$CI` variable is the variable in which we will store the CodeIgniter super object; this allows us to load CodeIgniter resources (libraries, models, views, and so on) in our library. We'll only be using this to load and use the CodeIgniter Session library, however.

The `$connection` variable will contain the instance of the Facebook class. This will allow us to grab any necessary user data and perform any operations that we like, such as updating a user's status or sending a message to one of their friends.

The next few variables are pretty self-explanatory—they will hold our API Key and Secret Key.

The `$user` variable will be used to store all of the information about our user, including general details about the user such as their profile URL and their name. The `$user_id` variable will be used to store the user ID of our user.

Finally, the `$client` variable is used to store general information about our connection to Facebook, including the username of the user currently using the connection, amongst other things such as server addresses to query for things like photos.

Class constructor

Our class constructor has to do a few things in order to allow us to authenticate our users using Facebook Connect. Here's the code:

```
function Facebook_connect($data)
{

  $this->CI =& get_instance();

  $this->CI->load->library('session');

  $this->api_key = $data['api_key'];
  $this->secret_key = $data['secret_key'];

  $this->connection =
    new Facebook($this->api_key, $this->secret_key);
  $this->client = $this->connection->api_client;
  $this->user_id = $this->connection->get_loggedin_user();

  $this->_session();

}
```

The first line in our function should be new to everyone reading this book. The function `get_instance()` allows us to assign the CodeIgniter super object by reference to a local variable. This allows us to use all of CodeIgniter's syntax for loading libraries, and so on; but instead of using `$this->load` we would use `$this->CI->load`. But of course it doesn't just allow us to use the Loader—it allows us to use any CodeIgniter resource, as we normally would inside a Controller or a Model. The next line of code gives us a brilliant example of this: we're loading the session library using the variable `$this->CI` rather than the usual `$this`.

The next two lines simply set the values of the API key and Secret Application Key into a class variable so that we can reference it throughout the whole class. The `$data` array is passed into the constructor when we load the library in our Controller. More on that when we get there.

Next up, we create a new instance of the Facebook Class (this is contained within the Facebook library that we include before our own class code) and we pass the API Key and Secret Application Key through to the class instance. This is all assigned to the class variable `$this->connection`, so that we can easily refer to it anywhere in the class.

The next two lines are specific parts of the overall `Facebook` instance. All of the client details and the data that helps us when using the connection are stored in a class variable, in order to make it more accessible. We store the client details in the variable `$this->client`. The next line of code stores all of the details about the user that were provided to us by the `Facebook` class. We store this in a class variable for the same reason as storing the client data: it makes it easier to get to. We store this data in `$this->user_id`.

The next line of code calls upon a function inside our class. The underscore at the beginning tells CodeIgniter that we only want to be able to use this function inside this class; so you couldn't use it in a Controller, for example. I'll go over this function shortly.

_session();

This function manages the user's CodeIgniter session. Take a look at the following code:

```
function _session()
{
  $user = $this->CI->session->userdata('facebook_user');

  if($user === FALSE && $this->user_id !== NULL)
  {
    $profile_data = array('uid','first_name', 'last_name',
      'name', 'locale', 'pic_square', 'profile_url');
    $info = $this->connection->api_client->
      users_getInfo($this->user_id, $profile_data);

    $user = $info[0];

    $this->CI->session->set_userdata('facebook_user', $user);
  }
  elseif($user !== FALSE && $this->user_id === NULL)
  {
    $this->CI->session->sess_destroy();
  }

  if($user !== FALSE)
  {
    $this->user = $user;
  }
}
```

This function initially creates a variable and sets its value to that of the session data from the CodeIgniter session library.

Then we go through a check to see if the session is empty and the `$this->user_id` variable is false. This means that the user has not yet logged in using Facebook Connect. So we create an array of the data that we want to get back from the `Facebook` class, and then use the function `users_getInfo()` provided by the class to get the information in the array that we created. Then we store this data into the `$user` variable and create a new session for the user.

The next check that we do is that if the `$user` variable is not empty, but the `$this->user_id` variable is empty, then the user is not authenticated on Facebook's side so we should destroy the session. We do this by using a function built in to the Session Library `sess_destroy();`

Finally, we check to see if the `$user` variable is not equal to `FALSE`. If it passes this check, we set the `$this->user` class variable to that of the local `$user` variable.

Final library code

Here is the full library code in context:

```
<?php

require_once(APPPATH . 'libraries/facebook/facebook.php');

class Facebook_connect
{
  var $CI;
  var $connection;

  var $api_key;
  var $secret_key;
  var $user;
  var $user_id;
  var $client;

  function Facebook_connect($data)
  {

    $this->CI =& get_instance();

    $this->CI->load->library('session');
```

```
        $this->api_key = $data['api_key'];
        $this->secret_key = $data['secret_key'];

        $this->connection =
          new Facebook($this->api_key, $this->secret_key);
        $this->client = $this->connection->api_client;
        $this->user_id = $this->connection->get_loggedin_user();

        $this->_session();

    }

    function _session()
  {
    $user = $this->CI->session->userdata('facebook_user');

    if($user === FALSE && $this->user_id !== NULL)
    {
      $profile_data = array('uid','first_name', 'last_name',
        'name', 'locale', 'pic_square', 'profile_url');
      $info = $this->connection->api_client->
        users_getInfo($this->user_id, $profile_data);

      $user = $info[0];

      $this->CI->session->set_userdata('facebook_user', $user);
    }
    elseif($user !== FALSE && $this->user_id === NULL)
    {
      $this->CI->session->sess_destroy();
    }

    if($user !== FALSE)
    {
      $this->user = $user;
    }
  }

  }

  ?>
```

The Controller

The Controller is where all of our logic will go. The Controller that we use for our Facebook authentication will need to call upon the Facebook Connect Wrapper, set some local variables for some user information, and load a view file. The view file will contain special HTML elements to show Facebook information. These tags are known as **Facebook Markup Language (FBML)**. We'll go over FBML briefly after this section.

```
<?php

class Facebooker extends Controller
{

  function Facebooker()
  {
    parent::Controller();

    $this->load->helper('url');
  }

  function index()
  {
    $data['api_key'] = "";
    $data['secret_key'] = "";

    $this->load->library('facebook_connect', $data);

    $data['user'] = $this->facebook_connect->user;
    $data['user_id'] = $this->facebook_connect->user_id;

    $this->load->view('facebook', $data);
  }

}
?>
```

As you can see, the Controller is fairly short and isn't as complex a way of authenticating users as Twitter oAuth (generating keys, and so on). I have named the Controller "Facebooker" because the class name "Facebook" has already been used for the core Facebook Client. If I had called the Controller Facebook there would be no output to the browser after a PHP failure. You should copy this code and save it in the `system/application/controllers/` folder as `Facebooker.php`.

In the class constructor, we load the URL Helper. We use the URL Helper in the view file to tell Facebook the location of our application.

The first thing that we do in the index function is to declare two array keys: one for our API Key and another for the Secret Application Key. You should set these to the keys that you received from Facebook when you created a new application. We subsequently load the Facebook Connect Wrapper library, and pass the `$data` array containing our API key and Secret Application Key to it.

The next two lines add to our `$data` array, this time adding the user and user ID information. On the final line we load the view file and pass the `$data` array to it.

The View file

The View file is very important to us and needs some explaining. As you would expect from a Facebook Connect application, the logo will be placed on the web page. A pop-up box will appear when you click on it, allowing you to log in to Facebook and allow access to the application. To do this however, you need to know FBML. FBML is a superset of HTML and adds on to HTML's features, basically letting you easily add Facebook specific details. The example application is immensely simple, but it gives you a quick look at FBML, giving you an idea of what it can do and how it does it.

```
<!DOCTYPE html>
<html xmlns="http://www.w3.org/1999/xhtml" xmlns:fb="http://www.
facebook.com/2008/fbml">
<head>
  <title>Facebook Connect</title>
</head>
<body>
  <script src="http://static.ak.connect.facebook.com/js/api_lib/v0.4/
FeatureLoader.js.php" type="text/javascript"></script>
  <?php if ( !$user_id ): ?>
    <fb:login-button onlogin="window.location='<?=current_url()?>'">
      </fb:login-button>
  <?php else: ?>
    <p><img class="profile_square" src="<?=$user['pic_square']?>" />
    Hi <?=$user['first_name']?>!</p>
    <p><a href="#" onclick="FB.Connect.logout(function()
      { window.location='<?=current_url()?>' });
        return false;" >(Logout)</a></p>

    <p>You are now logged in!!</p>
  <?php endif; ?>
```

```
    <script type="text/javascript">
      FB.init("<?php echo $api_key; ?>", "/xd_receiver.htm");
    </script>
  </body>
  </html>
```

As you can see, this is just a normal HTML document. We start off with a `DOCTYPE` declaration, open our `html` and `head` tags, set a page `title` and open our `body` tag. After this, though, we're in FBML territory.

The first thing that I have done is load in a JavaScript file so we can make use of all the Facebook Connect objects. Yes, I should do this in the `<head>` as opposed to after the `<body>` tag, but I've put it here to group all of the Facebook-specific stuff together.

In the following snippet of code, all I want to go through is the part that shows the Facebook Connect login button if a user is not logged in.

```
<?php if ( !$user_id ): ?>
<fb:login-button
  onlogin="window.location='<?=current_url()?>'">
</fb:login-button>
```

The first line is just a simple PHP `if` statement. If the variable `$user_id` is not set, we show the login button. Let's take a closer look at the code behind adding the login button.

Firstly you should notice that the tag we are using, it's an `<fb>` tag. You should also notice that there is a colon in the tag, followed by a string to describe the object that we want to place on the web page—in this case it is the `login-button`. Then we set an attribute `onlogin`, which sets the redirect page to the one we are currently on; once a user is authenticated they'll still be on the same page. The `current_url()` function is part of the URL Helper that we loaded in the Controller constructor. Finally, we close the login button tag `</fb:login-button>`.

There isn't much to digest here, considering the operations behind this single button. All you need to take away from this section are the following points:

- Facebook tags begin with `<fb` preceded by a colon and a string describing what you are adding to the page
- Tags end the same as any HTML tag. The ending tags open with a `</` instead of a `<`
- Tags can have attributes

The next part of the code determines what happens when a user is logged in. Obviously we don't want to show a logged in user the login button! Instead, we will display their profile picture, print the text "Hi!" followed by their first name, and then show a logout link.

```
<?php else: ?>
    <p><img class="profile_square" src="<?=$user['pic_square']?>" />
    Hi <?=$user['first_name']?>!<p>
    <p><a href="#" onclick="FB.Connect.logout(function()
      { window.location='<?=current_url()?>' });
        return false;" >(Logout)</a></p>

  <p>You are now logged in!!</p>
  <?php endif; ?>
```

To begin with, we are simply following our initial `if` statement with an `else`. (Note that we are using shorthand PHP.) Next, we use an image tag to show the users profile picture. We add in the welcoming text and echo out the user's first name. Then we show the user a logout link.

The logout link uses the JavaScript `onclick` event to call a function (contained within the JS file that we loaded from Facebook), which logs the user out. Just like when showing the login button, we also send along the `window.location` as the current URL, so that the user will be sent back to this page after logging out. We also show the user a short message telling them they are now logged in.

The final part to the view file is simply including a JavaScript file. Notice that we are sending the string `/xd_receiver.htm` as a parameter. This is a file that we need to add to our CodeIgniter application so that we can make use of the JavaScript Library provided by Facebook.

```
<script type="text/javascript">
    FB.init("<?php echo $api_key; ?>", "/xd_receiver.htm");
</script>
```

The file `xd_receiver.html` is a Cross Domain Communication Channel that allows us to us the JavaScript Library that Facebook has provided for us. The file should be placed at the root of our application—in the same folder as CodeIgniter's `index.php` file—so that it can be easily accessed. The file should contain the following code:

```
<!DOCTYPE html>
<html xmlns="http://www.w3.org/1999/xhtml" >
  <head>
    <title>Cross-Domain Receiver Page</title>
  </head>
  <body>
    <script
src="http://static.ak.facebook.com/js/api_lib/v0.4/XdCommReceiver.js"
type="text/javascript">
    </script>
  </body>
</html>
```

The only difference between the previous code and the code that Facebook provides directly is the differing doctypes. I have used an HTML5 doctype, whereas Facebook uses an XHTML 1.0 Strict doctype in the example shown on their developer wiki.

Now that you have added this file, you can go ahead and login with Facebook Connect!

Summary

There you have it—user authentication using Twitter oAuth and Facebook Connect. There are many similarities in how these systems work, but for us developers they both work slightly differently; Twitter makes us jump through hoops, and Facebook handles it all for us.

In the next chapter, we will go through Application Security—more specifically what CodeIgniter does to protect you, and some of the most common ways that a user can compromise your site, as well as how you can take preventative measures to stop them.

6
Application Security

Ensuring that your application is as secure as is humanly possible is no mean feat. There are so many that ways your application can be compromised that it's often difficult to keep your application locked down all of the time. However, there are steps that you can easily take to reduce the chances of anybody with some technical knowledge to gain unauthorized access to your application, or parts of or all of your databases.

CodeIgniter handles some of these steps, and you won't need to do anything to make use of them; they'll always be there. However, some of its defenses need to be turned on, or an action needs to happen for you to take full advantage of them. We have already touched upon this with the XSS Filter: it can be turned on permanently or it can be used on a case-by-case basis for each form field.

We will discuss the following topics in this chapter:

- URI security
- Global security
- Filtering data
- Password salting
- Database security
- Cross-site scripting

CodeIgniter's defenses

CodeIgniter comes with built-in security filters; some of these filters are by convention, and some need to be configured. We'll go over some of these now.

URI security

To refresh your memory, a URI is everything that comes after your web address. When using CodeIgniter, you will have a URI that looks like this:

```
index.php/controller/method/parameters
```

As a security precaution, CodeIgniter only allows certain characters in your URIs. You may only have the following characters in your URIs. You can change this in your `application/config/config.php` file, to add or remove any characters that should be allowed in your URIs; characters such as:

- Lowercase and Uppercase letters
- Numbers (0—9)
- Tilde (~)
- Underscore (_)
- Dash (-)
- Period (.)
- Colon (:)

Why does CodeIgniter use URIs?

CodeIgniter favors URI segments to map URLs to Controller files for one simple reason. Using other methods—such as building query strings—is not search engine friendly and also creates some security issues.

For example, you can get the URI string by using PHP quite simply as follows:

```
$uri = $_SERVER['REQUEST_URI'];
echo $uri;
```

This is a pretty safe method. However, if you were to use query strings, in most cases you would be using the `$_GET` variable to find this information. Using `$_GET` poses its own security problems, such as giving users the possibility to load scripts from outside the domain and run them on your own server. CodeIgniter does give you an option to enable query strings, but this is disabled by default.

On another note, URI strings are more search engine friendly and are also more readable for your site's visitors. There is no question that URIs are more user-friendly and are easier to read. Take a look at an example website URL, given next. The first is in the CodeIgniter URI style and the second is in the older query string based style. Both URLs would take you to the same page full of products in a web shop, but they both look totally different.

```
www.example.com/index.php/product/page/1
```

```
www.example.com/?c=product&m=page
```

CodeIgniter allows you to use query strings, and by default the trigger to set the controller name is **c** and the trigger for method names is **m**.

Why does CodeIgniter restrict URI characters?

There are a few reasons as to why CodeIgniter restricts what you can and cannot put into your URI segments.

Firstly, by allowing characters such as an asterisk (*) or quotations—either single quotes or double quotes—CodeIgniter is effectively allowing SQL statements to be passed into a function or used as input, as these characters feature heavily in SQL. If an SQL query were to be passed through a function and run against your database, you would be at risk of having someone delete or corrupt your database. Only allowing certain characters eliminates this risk.

Secondly, if these types of characters were to be allowed in your URI strings, you would have to sanitize all parameters passed to all functions where you accept them. This places an unwanted burden on you as a CodeIgniter developer to complete a task that would usually be expected of the framework.

Finally, by allowing characters into the controller and model segments that are not allowed in a PHP class name or function name, you are effectively disallowing CodeIgniter to map to a correct class or function. For this reason, CodeIgniter only allows the characters that can be used in a class name or function name to be used in URL strings, as anything else will result in a fatal PHP error.

Global data

Because CodeIgniter does not allow query strings to be used by default, the Input and Security Class unsets the `$_GET` array during initialization of the system.

All global variables are unset during system initialization, except those found in the `$_COOKIE` and `$_POST` arrays. This is effectively the same as turning `register_globals` off.

Global variables have always been a very high security risk, as global variables can be overwritten by using malicious scripts. This can allow users to change the way that your application was intended to be run and alter the way it works. For example, an overwritten global variable can allow a user to bypass a registration process and gain unauthorized access to your application.

`register_globals` has been turned off in PHP since version 4.2.0, but as CodeIgniter could be run on older versions or versions with `register_globals` specifically turned on, then it is best to carry out this security measure without making assumptions about the type of system that CodeIgniter will be run on.

Best practices

Before accepting any type of data into your application, whether it be from a form submission, COOKIE data, URI data, or even SERVER data, you are encouraged by the user guide to follow this three step guide:

1. Filter the data as if it were tainted
2. Validate the data to ensure that it is as expected (correct length, type, size, and so on)
3. Escape the data before inserting it into your Database

Filtering data

We have touched upon the XSS filter previously. CodeIgniter provides an excellent XSS Filter that filters data for any commonly used techniques for inserting malicious JavaScript code, or other types of code, into your application.

You can filter all types of data through the XSS Filter by opening up the file `/system/application/config/config.php` and setting the following variable:

```
$config['global_xss_filtering'] = TRUE;
```

Or you can filter data separately, by using the next function:

```
$data = $this->input->xss_clean($data);
```

Validation

We have already discussed validating data, previously. The Form Validation Library is the best tool that CodeIgniter offers for ensuring that the submitted data is of the correct type, size and even length. We have gone through this at length in *Chapter 4, User Authentication 1*, so there is no need to go through this again.

Escaping data

We have touched upon the functions for escaping data that are built in to the Active Record portion of the Database library. You can also escape data by using the function:

```
$this->db->escape();
```

which can be used when performing an SQL query using this function:

```
$this->db->query();
```

We'll go into this in much more detail later on in the chapter.

Strong password policies

You should make sure that your users always have a strong password. It is very easy to create a password policy with CodeIgniter, by using the Form Validation Library.

For example, you can set the minimum and maximum length of the password field. You can also easily make sure that the data entered in the password field and password confirmation field are the same.

An example password policy could be:

- Minimum length 6 characters
- Maximum length 12 characters
- Must be alpha-numeric characters, no symbols
- Must not be very commonly-used passwords
- Must not be the person's name
- Must not be the person's username

The advantages of having a strong password policy is that users will be aware of the security implications once they have an error saying that their password is too short. If you check the password to ensure it is not the same as the username, not "password", "1234", the user's name, or anything else that could be deemed inappropriate, then you can give a valid and helpful error message.

You could also go one step further and include a password strength meter, and only allow a user to have a strong password as deemed by the meter. Password strength meters are usually coded using JavaScript, so we won't delve into this.

Example Form Validation Library rules

Here's what the validation rules might look like for the password policy stated previously:

```
$this->form_validation->set_rules('name', 'First Name', 'required');
$this->form_validation->
  set_rules('username', 'Username', 'required');
$this->form_validation->
  set_rules('password', 'Password',
    'required|min_length[6]|max_length[12]|alpha_numeric|
    callback_not_obvious|callback_not_name|callback_not_username');

$this->form_validation->
  set_rules('password_conf', 'Password Confirmation',
    'required|matches[password]');
```

You'll notice that we make use of three callbacks. `not_obvious()` will be a function to determine if the password is one of the top five most commonly-used passwords. `not_name()` will determine whether the password is the persons name or not. `not_username()` will determine whether the password is the person's username or not. Let's create those functions.

```
function not_obvious($password)
{
  switch($password)
  {
    case "qwerty":
      $this->form_validation->
        set_message('not_obvious', 'The password provided is one of
the most used passwords, please try a more obscure password.');
      return FALSE;
      break;

    case "123456":
      $this->form_validation->
        set_message('not_obvious', 'The password provided is one of
the most used passwords, please try a more obscure password.');
      return FALSE;
      break;

    case "letmein":
      $this->form_validation->set_message('not_obvious', 'The password
provided is one of the most used passwords, please try a more obscure
password.');
      return FALSE;
```

```
            break;

        case "123":
            $this->form_validation->
              set_message('not_obvious', 'The password provided is one of
the most used passwords, please try a more obscure password.');
            return FALSE;
            break;

        case "password":
            $this->form_validation->
              set_message('not_obvious', 'The password provided is one of
the most used passwords, please try a more obscure password.');
            return FALSE;
            break;
    }

    return TRUE;

    }
```

This function is fairly repetitive. Basically, it checks that the password string provided does not match any of the five most common passwords. If a given password matches one of the top five, then an error message will be set and the function will return FALSE and break out of the loop.

The next function is `not_name()`, where we check to see if the password is the person's name.

```
function not_name($password)
{
  $name = set_value('name');

  if($name !== $password)
{
    return TRUE;
}
  else
{
    $this->form_validation->
      set_message('not_name', 'You user password provided was your
name. For security reasons we do not allow this.');
    return FALSE;
}
}
```

There is a function in here that might be new to you. `set_value()` allows you to grab the value of another one of the fields, provided that there are rules set for it to allow the Form Validation Library to handle it. This function checks to see if the password is the same as the name; if they are different we simply return `TRUE`, but if they are the same we set an error message and return `FALSE`.

The final callback function that we are going to write works in the same way as the previous one. The only difference is that we are checking whether the password is the same as the username this time, instead of the name.

```
function not_username($password)
{
  $username = set_value('username');

  if($username !== $password)
{
    return TRUE;
}
  else
{
    $this->form_validation->
      set_message('not_name', 'You user password provided was the same
as your username. For security reasons we do not allow this.');
    return FALSE;
}
}
```

Storing passwords securely

User passwords are quite possibly the most important data that you store on your server, so you should ensure that you have taken reasonable steps to store these securely. We'll go over some of the different methods that you can use to store passwords in a secure manner.

Storing hashes

Storing a password as a hash is possibly the easiest way to store user passwords, and is used by many websites. Most developers would go straight to using an MD5 hash because it is the most well-known of the types of hashing available to developers. However, I would recommend you use sha1 hashes, because these are longer than MD5 and have proved harder to find the plaintext to than MD5 hashes.

Hashing a password using sha1

There are two ways to hash a password using this method. Firstly, if your PHP installation supports it (the chances are that it will) then you will be able to use the function `sha1()` — this is the easiest way to hash a password. The second way is done in exactly the same way but instead uses a function provided by CodeIgniter, for the cases where sha1 is not available on your server.

The sha1() function

The process is brilliantly simple. Once a password has been given to you by the user — usually via a form — then you simply pass this value to the first parameter of the sha1 function.

```
$password = '1234';
$hash = sha1($password);
```

You can now store the password in the database safe in the knowledge that you have made it much more difficult for somebody to find the user passwords if they were somehow able to get hold of your database.

The $this->encrypt->sha1() function

This function is provided by CodeIgniter and is available to the developers out there who might not have sha1 available on their server. It works in exactly the same way as before, the only difference is that it doesn't use the native `sha1()` function.

Load the library

The first thing that you have to do to use this function is to load the CodeIgniter Encryption Library. This is the Library that holds the sha1 function. Here's how you load it:

```
$this->load->library('encryption');
```

Hash the password

This is done in the exact same way as hashing a password using the native function. The only difference is that instead of using `sha1()` you would use `$this->encrypt->sha1();`.

```
$password = '1234';
$hash = $this->encrypt->sha1($password);
```

Both functions will provide the exact same resulting hash. The only difference is that one function is native to the language and one is native to the framework.

Static salting

The next step up from hashing passwords is to salt your password hashes. This is the process of adding a string to a password to change its end hash, which will be completely different from the original password hash. Let's take a look at a few examples of how to do this.

When using salts, remember to salt the user password in exactly the same way, each time you need to check it against a database. This means that every time a user logs in, you need to salt the password in the same way, or else you won't be able to verify the password, even if it is typed in correctly.

Simple salts

Here's something I will call a 'simple' salt. This is where you put a salt string at the beginning or end of the password, then hash it.

```
$salt = '123456789987654321';
$password = 'password';

$start_hash = sha1($salt . $password);
$end_hash = sha1($password . $salt);
```

Complex salts

Once again I'm giving this my own name. A complex salt is where you split the password up somewhere, and add the salt in the middle. You should have strict password rules set up by using the Form Validation Library, so you should know how long the shortest password is so you don't split it at the last character.

Split at second character

You can split a password from every second character as follows:

```
$salt = '123456789987654321';
$password = 'pass';

$password_array = str_split($password, 2);
```

The contents of `$password_array` will look something like this.

```
Array
(
  [0] => pa
  [1] => ss
)
```

Now, to add the salt you would simply use:

```
$hash = sha1($password_array[0] . $salt . $password_array[1]);
```

Here's the code for clarity:

```
$salt = '123456789987654321';
$password = 'pass';

$password_array = str_split($password, 2);

$hash = sha1($password_array[0] . $salt . $password_array[1]);
```

Split the password in the middle

We can easily split the password in the middle, no matter how long or short the password is, by finding the length of the password and then dividing that by two to get our split point.

```
$salt = '123456789987654321';
$password = 'password';

$password_length = length($password); // int 8
$split_at = $password_length / 2; // int 4

$password_array = str_split($password, $split_at);

$hash = sha1($password_array[0] . $salt . $password_array[1]);
```

In the previous code snippet, the first two lines are simple; we're just setting values for our salt and the user password. The next line lets us find the length of the password; in this case its value will be 8. The next line is where we find the middle of the string; in this case its value will be 4. So we split the password variable up at the fourth character, as set in the `$split_at` variable. The next line is the same as before; we're simply adding a salt in the middle of the password.

You could create a function out of this so that you won't have to repeat yourself over and over. In fact, let's build a CodeIgniter plugin.

Create a new file inside the `system/application/plugins/` folder, called `hash_pi.php`.

Now paste the following code into this file:

```
<?php

function hash_password($password, $salt)
{
$password_length = length($password);
$split_at = $password_length / 2;

$password_array = str_split($password, $split_at);

$hash = sha1($password_array[0] . $salt . $password_array[1]);

return $hash;
}

?>
```

To use the plugin, you have to load it into one of your Controllers, as follows:

```
$this->load->plugin('hash');
```

Then you can simply use the function in a procedural way:

```
$hashed_password = hash_password($password, $salt);
```

Dynamic salting

Dynamic salting is just like using a static salt, except that the salt is different for every user, and is stored inside the database. Of course, if somebody were to grab a copy of the database, they would have the hashes and the salt. This is why we use both static salts and dynamic salts together. A dynamic salt is usually a random number, as this is easy to generate with PHP.

Simple dynamic salts

A simple dynamic salt is when you have a salt at either end of the password. For example, we could have the dynamic salt at the front of the password and the static salt at the end:

```
$static_salt = '123456789987654321';
$dynamic_salt = mt_rand();
$password = 'password';

$hash = sha1($dynamic_salt . $password . $static_salt);
```

This is pretty simple stuff. All you need to do is store the dynamic salt inside the database when you generate the salt for the first time (that is, at user registration) so that you can use it to check the user password when they log in to your website.

Complex dynamic salts

A complex dynamic salt is where we split the password up and put a salt in the middle, and one at the end. Of course you don't need to do it this way; you could split the password up however you like, and place the salt wherever you like—I'm just doing it this way because it's easier.

We'll re-use the code from the plugin that we made earlier, and update it.

```
<?php

function hash_password($password, $static_salt)
{
  $dynamic_salt = mt_rand();
$password_length = length($password);
$split_at = $password_length / 2;

$password_array = str_split($password, $split_at);

$hash = sha1($password_array[0] . $static_salt . $password_array[1] .
$dynamic_salt);

return $hash;
}

?>
```

The difference here is that we place the `$static_salt` variable in the middle and the `$dynamic_salt` at the end. We could've split the password anywhere, as many times as we liked, and rearranged it to make it even more secure. But this way is simple and we didn't need to change all that much.

Encrypting passwords

The CodeIgniter Encryption class provides a two way method of data encryption. You are able to store user passwords and retrieve them again. Using the Encryption class can be useful as it can provide resulting password strings that look much different to an `md5` or `sha1` hashed password. This can throw off many potential crackers at first sight. If a cracker has access to your database, there is no way to decrypt the user passwords unless you store your key in the database. Overall, the Encryption library provides a high level of security when compared to a simple hashing algorithm.

Setting an encryption key

To take full advantage of the potential of this library, you need to set an encryption key. Your key should be 32 characters long, with both uppercase and lowercase letters, numbers, and symbols. This should be as random as possible, so you should use a generator for this.

You store your key in the `/system/application/config/config.php` file. All you need to do is set the following array key:

```
$config['encryption_key'] = "YOUR KEY";
```

It is imperative that you keep your key as secret as possible. Should somebody find this key then they will be able to decode the strings easily.

Message length

You should take note that the encryption process will make the password roughly 2.6 times longer than the plain text password. You should bear this in mind when choosing to store passwords in a cookie (if it is imperative that the password is stored in a cookie and not in a more secure way, such as a session) as they can only hold 4K of data.

Loading the class

Before we can actually use the Encryption class we must first load it into one of our Controllers. This is the same as loading any other class in CodeIgniter:

```
$this->load->library('encrypt');
```

As always, once loaded we can use the library by using the `$this->encrypt` method.

Encoding passwords

Now that we have loaded the library, we can start encoding information! This is a fairly simple process.

```
$password = 'password';
$ciphertext = $this->encrypt->encode($password);
```

You can also pass in an Encryption key to the second parameter if you do not wish to use the one in your configuration file.

```
$password = 'password';
$key = 'veTadewEBE8a4Abatrat2e3TenaZusta';

$ciphertext = $this->encrypt->encode($password, $key);
```

Decoding passwords

You should never really need to decode user passwords. Nobody other than the user should know their password. Even if they forget it, they should simply be sent a new one. We'll go over how to decode information, for a full picture of the Encryption library.

Once again, as is the nature of CodeIgniter, everything is very simple.

```
$ciphertext = 'kdbvlkjasdbvlbdvbzkxbfsdfblkd';

$plaintext = $this->encrypt->decode($ciphertext);
```

We simply pass in the encrypted string—the cipher text—through to the `decode()` function, and assign the returned value—the plain text—to a variable, to allow us to reuse this elsewhere in our application.

Set mcrypt cipher

The Encryption Library uses the `mcrypt` PHP Library to encrypt information. The Encryption library allows you to set your preferred cipher, a list of which can be found on the PHP website at `http://www.php.net/manual/en/mcrypt.ciphers.php`.

```
$this->encrypt->set_cipher(MCRYPT_DES);
```

Database security

Another very important part of general application security is that of your database. Ensuring that your queries are all correct, that all data has been escaped before you use it in a query, and never ever trusting any user input will all help with safeguarding your database.

Escape queries

We have already been over the methods that CodeIgniter uses to escape your data, at the start of this chapter. This time around we'll go over how to escape the different parts of a query without CodeIgniter, as this is a skill that every developer should have.

Firstly, all database table names and field names should be escaped by using **backticks** (`). This will also avoid any issues where the name is a reserved word. This is especially useful when using a `WHERE` clause that uses the primary key `id` field. Here's an example:

```
SELECT * FROM `users` WHERE `username` = '$username' AND `id` = '$id'
```

Secondly, all variables that are included in a query should be properly escaped by using one of the methods shown at the beginning of this chapter.

The $this->db->escape() function

This function will determine the data type so that it can properly escape only string data. It will automatically add single quotes around the data so you don't have to. Here's how you would use it:

```
$sql = "INSERT INTO table (name)
  VALUES(".$this->db->escape($name).")";
$this->db->query($sql);
```

The $this->db->escape_str() function

This function will escape all data, regardless of type. In most cases you will be using the previous function rather than this one. In any case, here's how you use it:

```
$sql = "INSERT INTO table (name)
  VALUES(".$this->db->escape_str($name).")";
$this->db->query($sql);
```

The $this->db->escape_like_str() function

This function is useful when strings are used in the `LIKE` portion of your query. This enables the wildcards to be correctly escaped along with the string. Here's an example of its usage:

```
$like = 'adam';
$sql = "SELECT id FROM table
  WHERE column LIKE '%".$this->db->escape_like_str($like)."%'";
$this->db->query($sql);
```

Query bindings

Although data will be escaped using a bound query, CodeIgniter does it for you. Here is an example of how you would bind the values to your query:

```
$sql = "SELECT * FROM column
  WHERE id = ? AND name = ? AND group = ?";
$this->db->query($sql, array(1, 'adam', 'administrators');
```

In short, query binding allows you to write a query and bind certain values to it for later use. Query bindings will also significantly simplify your SQL strings; this can be a huge benefit if you have long queries.

Limiting account access

You should create a new user account for your database each time a new application has specific needs. For example, if you use the root account for an application, but you are only performing read, write, and delete operations then you will not need the ability to create, edit, or remove tables.

The reasoning behind doing this is that if somebody were to gain access to your database and were able to run queries on it, they would not be able to drop the tables, as MySQL (or whatever database you use) will limit the types of query that the user account can make.

The main case for this point would be SQL Injection. **SQL Injection** is where a string such as 'OR', or '= ', is inserted into a form or a URL where it will be run on the database. This will usually return an error message that can be used by the malicious user to return a dump of part or all of your database. If you haven't properly escaped your queries then a user could run a query like this on your database:

```
SELECT * FROM `users` WHERE `id` = 14; DROP TABLE `users`
```

This would allow them to completely drop the users table from the database. But by limiting the access to the database account we can completely stop this from happening, as the query will not be able to run correctly.

Cross-site scripting (XSS)

Cross-site scripting (**XSS**) is a way of injecting malicious JavaScript code into your application. This type of exploit can be used to hijack a user's cookie, which can effectively let the user who injected the code take the ID of any user on your website, simply by linking them to your site with the code added in.

CodeIgniter comes with an XSS Filter, and can be turned on to run all the time. We discussed this at the beginning of the chapter. You can also run POST data through the XSS Filter on a case-by-case basis. You do this by passing the Boolean TRUE to the second parameter of the post function.

```
$this->input->post('username'); // not filtered
$this->input->post('password', TRUE); // filtered
```

You can also use the XSS filter as a rule with the Form Validation Library. Just set the last rule to be `xss_clean`.

Changing the default file structure

Changing the way that your application works can be a good way to secure your application. With CodeIgniter you can rename your system folder and even place it above the web root, making it inaccessible from a browser window. You can rename your application folder and pull it out of the system folder. Doing this may keep your application more secure than by simply keeping the default structure. The main reason behind this is that if vulnerability were to be found in the CodeIgniter core then nobody could act upon it, because you would have renamed your system folder and it won't be accessible to him or her anyway. Renaming your application folder keeps people from easily identifying it as a CodeIgniter project, therefore limiting the ways they could try to breach the application.

Once you rename your application and system folders and move them both (application out of system, and system out of the web root), open up `index.php` and change the following variables:

```
$system_folder = "system";
$application_folder = "application";
```

Here's what you file structure should look like:

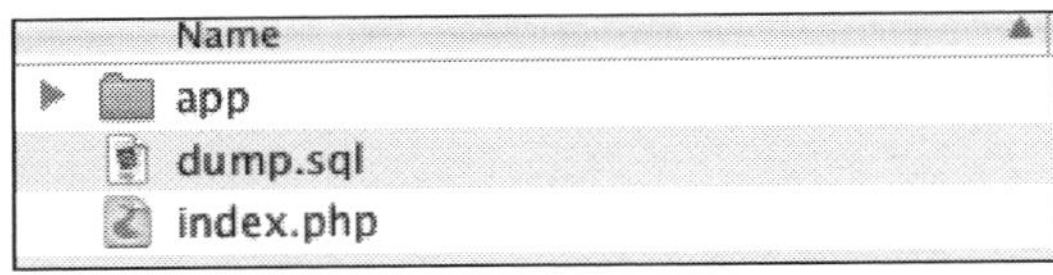

It's worth pointing out here that you can put your application folder pretty much anywhere, and CodeIgniter will find it for you. All you need to do is ensure that the name of your folder is the same as the variable you set in `index.php`.

Staying up-to-date

Remember to update your CodeIgniter applications and versions of PHP (if possible) to stay up-to-date and cover any security patches. By removing your system folder out of the web root, you are able to use one system folder for all of your applications; this makes it much easier to upgrade a number of applications at once with no fuss at all. Keep an eye on the CodeIgniter website and Twitter stream for the latest version updates.

Summary

This chapter has covered a range of areas that you can easily act upon in order to improve the security of your applications enormously. In the next chapter we'll go over the different areas in which you can improve your application in order to allow it to handle large amounts of traffic. Essentially, we'll go over the steps for building a large-scale application.

7
Building a Large-Scale Application

Being able to build and run a large-scale application is a great skill for any developer looking to broaden their horizons with freelancing opportunities, to build that web app you've always wanted to create or take CodeIgniter into a corporate setting. The techniques we'll be going through in this chapter can be applied to an application of any size, but the effects will be more noticeable on a larger application. We'll be going through the kinds of changes we need to make to the application for different hardware implementations or cloud storage.

In this chapter you will:

- Learn how to run benchmarks on your application
- Identify and rectify bottlenecks in your application
- Use the CodeIgniter Output Cache to cache view files
- Use the Database Library Query Cache to optimize SQL operations
- Build and utilize a memcache library to avoid disk activity
- Know the advantages and disadvantages of using multiple instances to balance load over your application

Running benchmarks

Benchmarks let you log the time it takes for a part, or multiple parts, of your application to run. For example, you could log the time it takes to log a user in. You should put benchmarks in the core of your application and anywhere else that you feel you would need to time so that you can make it run faster in the future.

Why run benchmarks?

We know how to run benchmarks and what they do. But why should we bother? Once you've benchmarked your application, you can generate a report by using the Benchmarking class. This allows you to easily see the timings of your application wherever you have set a benchmark. You can then seek out any bottlenecks in your application, and rectify them.

Where should I use benchmarks?

It is a good idea to benchmark your application as much as possible; this is useful because it allows you to look at very specific areas of your site. The CodeIgniter Benchmarking class is very good because it allows you to run benchmarks inside other benchmarks. This can be very useful if you want to run a benchmark for each of your Controller and Model functions, and allows you to run benchmarks for other, more specific parts of your application.

Ideally, you should benchmark anywhere that your application accessess data (your Models). Whenever you access the database, an API, RSS Feed, or other source of data, benchmark it. If you're using a third-party API or a third-party hosted RSS Feed, there might not be much you can do to speed things up; in some cases you can be put on a whitelist for access.

I would recommend benchmarking all of your database queries. This will enable you to look at how long every query takes to run and optimize them as needed.

Types of bottlenecks

A bottleneck is a part of your application that is slower than the other parts, and that is slowing down the application as a whole. In it's basic form, your application is the beer in a bottle, and the bottleneck is slowing your application flow. Here are a number of different types of bottlenecks, along with how to identify them and how to rectify the problem.

Database

A database bottleneck is where the database is delivering data slower than you'd like in your application.

Identifying a database bottleneck

Look at all of the benchmarks that you are running that encompass just database queries, and find the average load time for each query. You should be able to see the ones that take longer than the others, at a glance. Of course, if some of your queries are fairly long and some are fairly brief, then you should only look at the queries that are similar to any shown with a long load time.

Identifying a bottleneck in the database is easy, but identifying *why* it is a bottleneck isn't so easy. Sometimes the bottleneck may simply be a bad query. In other cases it could be a slow connection to the database server, or high latency. In any case, it is up to you to determine why a database issue has occurred.

Rectifying a database bottleneck

There are a few ways in which a database can be a problem for you. The first thing I do when I find a slow SQL query is immediately look at the query. If I can see a glaring problem with the query, then I can rectify it, and then, rerun the benchmarks, and have a look at the profiler. If the problem isn't fixed I look at other avenues.

Using the Active Record class will slow down your queries. If you can, you should try a query without using the Active Record class, just to see the difference. If this doesn't speed up the query, then it may well be a network problem between your database server and web server. If you are only on one server, then the server might be under a lot of load.

If you are seeing a lot of load on the database, I would suggest buying another server. You should use the same company for this server, as usually they do not charge for internal bandwidth. You can then set up this second server as a sole database server. This should give the database the extra resources it needs to run smoothly.

Alternatively, if you find that all of your database `SELECT` queries are returning the whole table, but you are only using a small subset of the table, then you should just return what you need. You can use the LIMIT clause to limit the number of rows you return, and even set an offset to get the correct area of your table. If you only use one row for some queries, then you should only be returning one row to use in the code.

Code

A code bottleneck is where your code is the weak link in the chain; it is running slower than all (or most) of the other resources in your application.

Identifying a code bottleneck

If your application has a fast database, the front-end files are minified (compressed or otherwise) and you have plenty of bandwidth available, then it is likely that your code is running slow. You have yourself a code bottleneck.

Look at the more general benchmarks that you have set for your application. You should be able to see where the code is lagging behind, and where the code is speedy. You should then open up the correct Controllers or Models where you are seeing this, to investigate more closely.

Rectifying a code bottleneck

There are a lot of different ways in which you can speed up your code.

Firstly, if you can use a native PHP functions but aren't, then you should be. Native PHP functions are going to run faster than your own brew or even the CodeIgniter functions. Of course, in some cases, there aren't any native PHP functions that do the same thing (an example of this would be all of the CodeIgniter libraries, helpers, and so on) so you have to take this into account, too.

Moreover, if there is a better native PHP function to use, then do so because better usually means faster. For example, navigate to the pages on `php.net` for the functions `rand()` and `mt_rand()` — `www.php.net/rand` and `www.php.net/mt_rand` respectively — and look at the descriptions of the functions.

rand

(PHP 4, PHP 5)

rand — Generate a random integer

mt_rand

(PHP 4, PHP 5)

mt_rand — Generate a better random value

Notice how the description for `mt_rand()` is"**Generate a better random value**"? There are many examples of this in the PHP language and many of those examples are quicker functions.

API

An API bottleneck is where you are pulling in data from an external source, by using a third-party API. An example of this could be a user's timeline on Twitter.

Identifying an API bottleneck

By looking at the benchmarks for the code that encompasses the API calls, you should be able to see how fast the code runs. If any particular API call is slower than the others for no particular reason, there may be a problem with the API itself. Of course, you'd have to take into account authenticated API calls versus non-authenticated API calls, as authenticated calls may take a little longer.

Rectifying an API bottleneck

There might not be anything that you can do to fix an issue with a third-party API. In some cases you can get whitelisted if you make a lot of calls to the API, so the company won't throttle your speed for using up too many resources. This is entirely up to the company who created and is maintaining the API, though. In this instance all you can do is contact them.

Bandwidth

Bandwidth is the allocated volume of data that you can send and receive from your server. This is usually an order of magnitude higher than the allocated web space that your hosting company gives you.

Identifying a bandwidth bottleneck

You can tell if you have a bandwidth bottleneck because the traffic going to your website will be much higher than the bandwidth allows, leaving some of your users with a blank screen; the server will just max out and use all of the bandwidth it has. If you use all of your bandwidth before the billing period on your hosting revolves (usually one month) you could incur extra charges.

Rectifying a database bottleneck

If users are reporting that they are seeing an empty screen, then there are two things that you can do to try to solve the problem.

Firstly, you can try to: minify your application; compress all your images; reduce the number of HTTP requests your app makes; use freely-available hosted versions of JavaScript libraries; anything that will cut down on the size of your application's pages. Any of these things will help to cut down bandwidth usage.

Secondly, and finally, if the bandwidth needs are genuinely much higher than is available to you, upgrade your hosting package. I would recommend moving to a cloud-based hosting service or an easily-expandable **Virtual Private Server** (**VPS**) or other similar service. As long as you can add and remove resources as and when you need to, you'll be in the clear with regards to bandwidth troubles.

Static

A static bottleneck is where the front end of your application is slowing the overall loading time. This is usually broken down into JavaScript, CSS, and image files.

Identifying a static bottleneck

There are a number of ways in which you can identify these types of bottlenecks. By far, the best way is to use **Browser Tools**. Safari comes with built-in developer tools that allow you to see the time that it took to load each item on the page. This enables you to see if any static content needs to be compressed.

Firefox also allows this functionality. You can install the YSlow! add-on from Yahoo!. This lets you see the time that each item on the page took to load. It also grades your website based on its performance, and gives you feedback on how you can get a better grade in the areas that you need to. There is also the opportunity to simply take all of that the images on the page and upload them to a compression site so that you can download them again, compressed. Google Chrome also has this functionality.

Rectifying a static bottleneck

There are many ways in which you can make your pages load faster. The first thing I would do is to place all of the JavaScript link tags or JavaScript code before the `body` tag of your website. This way, the server will not wait to download the scripts before the rest of the website. The user will see the website first and the scripts will load last; this means that the website is available much more quickly, especially if you have a lot of scripts, or if the scripts are fairly large.

The next thing I would do is to compress all of the static content, JavaScript, images, and CSS. You should always chose the correct file size for your images to ensure that they will load quickly. You could also try to use a sprite map. A **sprite map** is basically a set of related images all as one image; this lets you only use one HTTP request to download one file. To use the images you would simply use CSS to change the absolute positioning to the correct pixels where the corner or the different image might be on the spite map.

Another way that you can save some time on the page loading of your application is to use a **Content Delivery Network** (**CDN**). A CDN basically saves multiple copies of your images and other resources across many servers in different locations. So when a user comes to your website they load the static content closest to them, essentially eliminating the bottleneck in the method of using a single server to deliver everything.

Caching

Caching is an important part of the performance of any large-scale application. Without any type of cache, a large-scale application will need extra resources, which can be quite expensive if your application is CPU-intensive. Therefore, you should always take advantage of the tools that are available to you, which in our case is the CodeIgniter Output Cache.

How does it work?

The CodeIgniter Output Cache lets you turn on caching on a per-page basis. This means that you can essentially cache only the pages that take too long to load. When you turn caching on, you also set the time for which the cache should keep the cached page saved before refreshing it.

The first time that a user goes to the page, the output cache will save a cached copy of the page inside `/system/cache/` folder, and will serve it to the user. Every request for the page thereafter will simply serve up the cached page. If the cache has expired, however, then the cache will re-cache the page.

How long should I cache pages for?

You should set the expire time for your pages based on what the pages content is. If the page is the front page to a blog, and you only post once a week, set the expire time for a week from the time that you add a post. If your page is a user list for a web app and is heavily used, set it for a few minutes.

Using caching

The caching functionality of CodeIgniter is contained within the Output class. The Output class is instantiated when CodeIgniter loads, so there's no need to load anything special to use this.

To enable caching, put the following line of code anywhere inside one of your Controller functions. You should place this line of code in each function that you wish to be cached.

```
$this->output->cache(n);
```

The first (and only) parameter is the length of time for which you want to keep the cached page, specified in minutes.

Optimize SQL queries

You will most definitely need to optimize your SQL queries for use on a large-scale application. Here is a list of the things that you can do to speed them up.

Query caching

Query caching is a part of the CodeIgniter Database library, and allows you to store information in a text file on your server, essentially cutting out the database altogether.

To cache or not to cache?

There are many deciding factors on whether you should cache your queries or not, but generally it is a good idea to do this. A shared hosting environment will benefit more from query caching over a cloud-based system, as retrieving files across multiple servers can be an unwanted burden. Also, if your database is already highly optimized, you are unlikely to see a massive difference in speed—you're simply shifting the speed from a database retrieval system to a file system retrieval system.

Only `SELECT` queries are cacheable, as these queries are the only ones that produce a result, which can then be stored inside a file.

How query caching works

Every query that you run through the cache will have its own file inside a cache folder that you specify to CodeIgniter—the result of the query will then be stored inside the corresponding file. CodeIgniter will organize these files into sub-folders as needed.

Managing cache files

Because there is no way for cache files to expire, you will need to build in your own deletion routines into your application. For example, if you have a blog and you publish a new post, you will want to delete the cache files for your home page so that the new post will show up.

Using query caching

There are two functions that you need to be aware of to start using query caching. These are `$this->db->cache_on()` and `$this->db->cache_off()`. You guessed it; they turn the query cache on and off, respectively. You should wrap each of your queries with these two functions. Here's an example:

```
// Turn caching on
$this->db->cache_on();
$query = $this->db->query("SELECT * FROM table");

// Turn caching off for this one query
$this->db->cache_off();
$query = $this->db->query("SELECT * FROM users WHERE id ='$id");

// Turn caching back on
$this->db->cache_on();
$query = $this->db->query("SELECT * FROM table_2");
```

Deleting cache files

As was mentioned before, you need to build in routines to your application to delete cache files. Thankfully, CodeIgniter has included a function to help make that much easier to do.

Cache files are created according to the URI string of your site. Taking the example form the user guide, if your URI is `index.php/blog/comments/` then the sub-folder that your file will be stored in will be `blog+comments`. Therefore, to delete the file containing the cache queries, you would use the following line of code:

```
$this->db->cache_delete('blog','comments');
```

Deleting all cache files

CodeIgniter also has the ability to delete all of the cache files. This is a fairly simple process; just call the following function in one of your Controllers:

```
$this->db->cache_delete_all();
```

Limit results

If your queries look something like:

```
$this->db->query('SELECT * FROM table');
$this->db->get('table');
```

Then you might want to take a look at limiting your queries.

LIMIT clause

If you find these types of queries and you are not using all of the data, or are using only a single line, then you should consider limiting your queries. This will save on database overhead and will make your queries run much faster. This will also help to keep file size down, when used in conjunction with query caching. Utilizing the `LIMIT` clause of a query is also useful when using pagination.

```
$this->db->query('SELECT * FROM table LIMIT 10');

$this->db->limit(10);
$this->db->get('table');
```

I have provided two examples of the new query: one pure SQL statement and another using CodeIgniter's Active Record implementation.

Only select what you need

Another way to limit queries is to only select what you need. Take the following example of a database:

```
CREATE TABLE `users` (
`id` INT(11) PRIMARY KEY AUTO_INCREMENT,
`username` VARCHAR(255) NOT NULL,
`password` VARCHAR(255) NOT NULL,
`email` VARCHAR(255) NOT NULL,
`group` INT(11) NOT NULL,
`first_name` VARCHAR(255) NOT NULL,
`last_name` VARCHAR(255) NOT NULL
)
```

Let's say we are building a member list, and our query looks like this (Active Record):

```
$this->db->get('users');
// produces: SELECT * FROM users
```

If we only use the user's id, their username, their group and their email, then we can simply limit our query to only select that data:

```
$this->db->select('id, username, group, email');
$this->db->from('users')
$this->db->get();
// produces: SELECT id, username, group, email FROM users
```

Avoid disk activity

The slowest part of a web application is where a file is being retrieved; it is much quicker to access the data in memory than inside a file. Therefore you should always look at the option of using a library such as memcache or APC to cache your pages into memory, making it easier and quicker to get hold of them when they are needed.

You could take this a step further and cache pages by using the CodeIgniter Output Cache, and then cache those static pages into memory using memcache.

PHP has a memcache module available for installing. You should check with your host if this is available to you or if it can be installed, either by them or yourself.

Memcache example

Here is an example of how you would interface with the memcache library, using pure PHP.

```
<?php

$memcache = new Memcache;
$memcache->connect('localhost', 11211) or die ("Could not connect");

$tmp_object = new stdClass;
$tmp_object->str_attr ='test';
$tmp_object->int_attr = 123;

$memcache->set('key', $tmp_object, false, 10) or die ("Failed to save
data at the server");
echo"Store data in the cache (data will expire in 10 seconds)<br/>\n";

$get_result = $memcache->get('key');
echo"Data from the cache:<br/>\n";

var_dump($get_result);

?>
```

Let's go over this code before moving on. The first thing that we do is to create a new variable, `$memcache`, and assign it to a new instance of the memcache class. Then we connect to the memcache server on port 11211—the default port for memcache to listen to requests on. The next three lines of code simply create a variable and assign an object to it and give it two parameters. Then we immediately save the value of this variable to memcache. Finally we simply retrieve the data back again and echo it out.

Memcache CodeIgniter library

CodeIgniter allows us to create libraries for any purpose. In this instance, we will create a wrapper library that will let us use memcache by using the CodeIgniter syntax. We will also add debugging information to the library, to allow us to debug the code more easily using CodeIgniter logs, if needed.

Create a file called `memcached.php` inside `/system/application/libraries/` folder.

Constructor

As we want to be able to use the memcache library in our applications quickly, we will connect to the memache server in the constructor.

```
<?php

class Memcached
{

  var $memcache;

  function Memcached()
  {
    $this->memcache = new Memcache;
    $this->memcache->connect('localhost', 11211);
    log_message('debug','Created Memcache connection.');
  }

?>
```

This is fairly simple. Simply, we are creating a new memcache connection and logging a debug message stating that the connection has been created. The connection is always created on port 11211, as this is the default memcache port, as stated before. If your installation of memcache has it listening on another port, you should change this to reflect the correct port number.

Data functions

Here are our wrapper functions that deal with the data stored on the server:

```
function set($key, $data, $flag, $expires)
{
  $this->memcache->set($key, $data, $flag, $expires);
}

function replace($key, $data, $flag, $expires)
{
  $this->memcache->replace($key, $data, $flag, $expires);
}

function get($key, $flag)
{
  return $this->memcache->get($key, $flag);
}

function delete($key, $timeout)
{
  $this->memcache->delete($key, $timeout);
}
```

The first function allows us to set data on the server. The first and second parameters should be self-explanatory; we set a key to identify the data and then set the data. The flag that we set will usually be `0` but can be set to `MEMCACHE_COMPRESSED`, in order to store the data compressed.

The `replace` function works in exactly the same way as the `set` function, except that it will replace the data already stored by the key passed.

Moving on, we have a function that lets us retrieve the data that we have set already. The first parameter is the key that we use to set the data in the first place. The second parameter is where we pass `MEMCACHE_COMPRESSED`, to return the data compressed.

Finally, the delete function allows us to delete data from the memcache server. The first parameter is simply the key that we use to identify the data, and the second parameter is a timeout. This means that when this parameter set to 30, the data will be deleted after 30 seconds. This defaults to `0`.

Maintenance functions

There are two functions that allow us to maintain the memcache server. The first is `flush()`, which marks all memcache items as expired, allowing us to overwrite any occupied memory. The second is `close()`, which closes the connection to memcache.

```
function flush()
{
  $this->memcache->flush();
  sleep(1);
}

function close()
{
  $this->memcache->close();
  log_message('debug','Closed Memcache connection.');
}
```

We use the `sleep()` function to delay our application for one second. This is because we will not be able to write anything to memcache for a second, so we sleep whilst this period runs its course.

Full library code

Here is the full library code for clarity:

```
<?php

class Memcached
{

  var $memcache;

  function Memcached()
  {
    $this->memcache = new Memcache;
    $this->memcache->connect('localhost', 11211);
    log_message('debug','Created Memcache connection.');
  }

  function set($key, $data, $flag, $expires)
  {
    $this->memcache->set($key, $data, $flag, $expires);
  }
```

```
    function replace($key, $data, $flag, $expires)
    {
      $this->memcache->replace($key, $data, $flag, $expires);
    }

    function get($key, $flag)
    {
      return $this->memcache->get($key, $flag);
    }

    function delete($key, $timeout = 0)
    {
      $this->memcache->delete($key, $timeout);
    }

    function flush()
    {
      $this->memcache->flush();
      sleep(1);
    }

    function close()
    {
      $this->memcache->close();
      log_message('debug','Closed Memcache connection.');
    }

}

?>
```

Using the library

To use the library, simply load it into one of your Controllers, as follows:

```
$this->load->library('memcached');
```

Then you can use the functions as follows:

```
$this->memcached->set($key, $data, $flag, $expires);
```

Here is our example from before, but this time we're using the CodeIgniter library instead of the native PHP functions.

```
<?php

class Memcachetest extends Controller
{
  function Memcachetest()
  {
    parent::Controller();
    $this->load->library('memcached');
  }

  function index()
  {
    $tmp_object = new stdClass;
    $tmp_object->str_attr ='test';
    $tmp_object->int_attr = 123;

    $this->memcached->
      set('key', $tmp_object, false, 10)
        or die ("Failed to save data at the server");
    echo
"Store data in the cache (data will expire in 10 seconds)<br/>\n";

    $get_result = $this->memcached->get('key');
    echo"Data from the cache:<br/>\n";

    var_dump($get_result);

  }
?>
```

You can see that both examples are almost identical. The only difference is that instead of creating a memcache connection ourselves we have the library do it for us.

Run multiple application instances

You might want to think about running multiple instances of your application, either on the same server or spread across numerous servers.

Advantages

There are many ways in which you can benefit from having multiple instances of your application running across multiple servers.

Mainly, this will help to reduce the load and strain on any one part of your server. You will also be able to handle more requests by having more instances to handle them. Imagine buying a ticket at a cinema. If there is only one person selling tickets, it might take a while to serve everybody, and a queue is likely to form. If there are two or more people selling tickets at booths, then the people will get served much quicker and the queue is likely to be shorter. The same principle applies to web development; if there are more application instances then the application will scale better.

Of course, you couldn't just have 100 application instances and expect everything to speed up 100-fold. You'd need extra database resources, too. This would all depend on how your application works, though, and how you cache your database queries. If your queries are all file-system based then you would see an increase in performance, but probably not by as much. The trick is to find out what the best number of instances that you can run whilst still seeing an increase in performance.

Moreover, running multiple instances of your application will help when testing out new features. You could perform an update to one application and be able to essentially bucket test it. If you're using a version control system, then it will be easy to roll back to a previous commit if there is a problem.

If the application that you are running is a software platform, and each application instance is for a different customer, then you can make changes to the individual applications as needed. This could get messy, but as long as you keep the base application the same, there will be no problem with adding things for your clients on a per-client basis.

Disadvantages

Of course there are disadvantages as well as advantages to running many instances of your application.

The first thing that comes to mind is that you would need to write some kind of loading functionality that runs before CodeIgniter loads the application. In this case, you'll need to look at writing a hook to decide where to send the user. Writing the code to load from a different application isn't the hard bit, though; the hard part is deciding how to split the users up between the applications, in order to ensure that they use the same one throughout their session. One idea would be to set a piece of session data, or save a database record, so the loader always loads from the same application instance.

The easiest way to code this would be to hook into the system before the application is loaded. A `pre_system` hook is likely to be the best bet, although this could be done in a Controller—but then you would be complicating things more for yourself.

If you are also running multiple database instances, you will face a problem with syncing up the databases. If a user performs an action on one instance then comes back to the site later and they get directed to a different instance than before, then they expect everything to work the same. Therefore you will need to run a `cron` job periodically, to sync the different databases.

You could find it difficult managing multiple application instances, especially if you are using a version control system, as you could make a change to one application and you will have to copy everything to the other applications. Some version control systems make this easy for you, but others don't have an easy way to do it at all. This is something to think about when deciding whether or not to run multiple application instances.

Summary

There you have it—some of the best ways to streamline your application ready for enormous amounts of traffic. In the next chapter, we will take a look at web services, and how to open up your application to third-party developers, by using a REST server.

8
Web Services

The Web, as it stands now, is full of web services. You have probably heard of most of them. Websites such as Twitter provide a service where you can grab tweets from their APIs. Pretty much any website with an API can be described as a web service.

In this chapter we will:

- Learn about web services
- Learn what a RESTful web service is
- Learn how to build and interact with a RESTful web service
- Create a REST Server to make creating RESTful web services simple
- Create an extended Controller to abstract the REST implementation and allow us to focus on building the service

What is a web service?

The W3C describes a Web Service as "*a software system designed to support interoperable machine-to-machine interaction over a network*". This means that a connection can be established between two computers regardless of operating system or programming language. As long as both sides recognize the protocol used, they can communicate.

In short, a web service allows you to connect to it and perform queries on the data and functions that it holds just as if you were using the service on your own server. The service could be anything from a post code validation service to a blog that allows you to edit the contents from elsewhere.

Types of web service

There are a number of ways in which you can build a web service.

Remote procedure call

RPC web services provide a set of functions that interface to the application directly. Usually these services are simply a number of functions that have been set to do one task. This style of web service may be familiar to many web developers as it mimics the way models might work. The only difference is that the call is happening across the Internet.

CodeIgniter gives us a great set of libraries for using RPC, in the form of the XML-RPC Client and Server Libraries. **XML-RPC** is a specification and a set of implementations that allows software to communicate with a server by using the XML as the request.

Representational State Transfer

REST is a method which, rather than defining functions that can be used in applications, defines a resource—a URI—to be used to perform actions on.

REST simply uses the assets that the HTTP protocol has. By using `GET`, `POST`, `PUT`, and `DELETE` HTTP methods, we can distinguish between the different types of requests and deal with them accordingly. We'll be building a RESTful web service in this chapter.

RESTful web service

The first step in building a RESTful web service is to define what it is we want to provide a service to. To keep things simple, we'll create the web service for a blog. We'll be able to add, edit, delete, and get a list of all of the blog posts.

Defining the resource

Our resource will be located at `http://yourdomain.ext/index.php/`—this allows us to use the same URLs for our REST Web Service as for our actual web frontend.

The URI that we will be using to access our data is going to be from `http://yourdomain.ext/index.php/server/post/` and our client is going to be located at `http://yourdomain.ext/index.php/client/`. Now of course usually the web service will be on a different server to the client application, but in our case we'll be using the same server, and even the same application. We could use two CodeIgniter applications if we wanted to.

How it will work

Before we write any code, we need to go over how our REST web service will work.

The Client Controller acts as the client. This could be another CodeIgniter application on another server. In fact, it could even be a Rails or Django project on another server. As long as all requests are formatted in the way that the server expects, the language and environment doesn't matter at all. The client performs all requests and waits for the server to return something, whether this is returned data or just an OK message.

The client sends data to the server in the form of a serialized array. The library will format this as necessary, depending on what type of request you are making. The server (Post Controller) will send data back, also as an array.

The Post Controller works out what type of request is being made, and deals with it accordingly. In most cases, it is simply a call to a Model and sending the data back to the client.

All types of requests will be sent to the same server URL, `http://yourdomain.ext/index.php/server/post/`. We differentiate the different types of request on the server side by using a different function for each type of request: PUT, POST, GET, and DELETE. So the request made on the single URL will be routed automatically by the server to the relative function for the request type. So if we perform a GET request on the URL, the server will route us through to the function <cit>`post_get()`. We can extend this web service as far as we like, as long as we have four functions for each type. So we could change the second parameter to comments, and be able to perform actions on a theoretical comments table. We can also add in an ID to the third parameter of the URL to focus our actions on one post entry, such as retrieving a single post.

Creating our files

We're going to be using a number of different files to create our web service. Create two new Controller files called `Client.php` and `Server.php`.

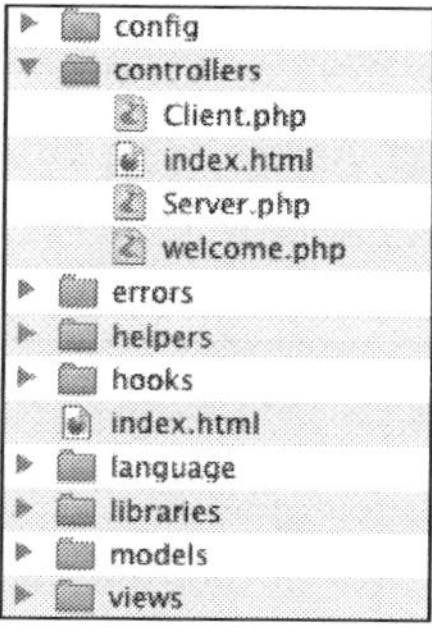

We will also be using a library. Create a new library file called `Rest.php`.

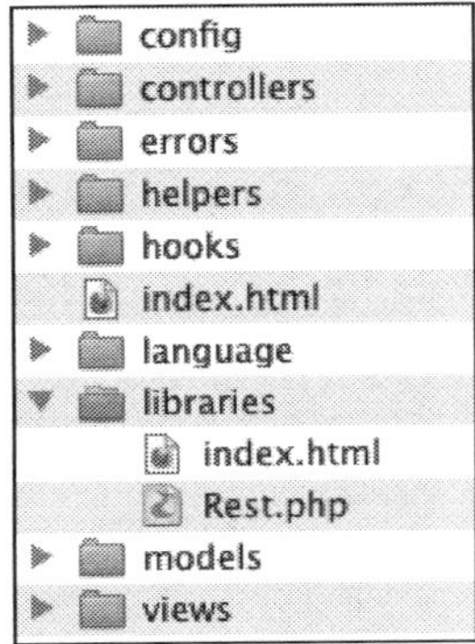

We will also be using a Model. Create a new Model file called `postmodel.php`.

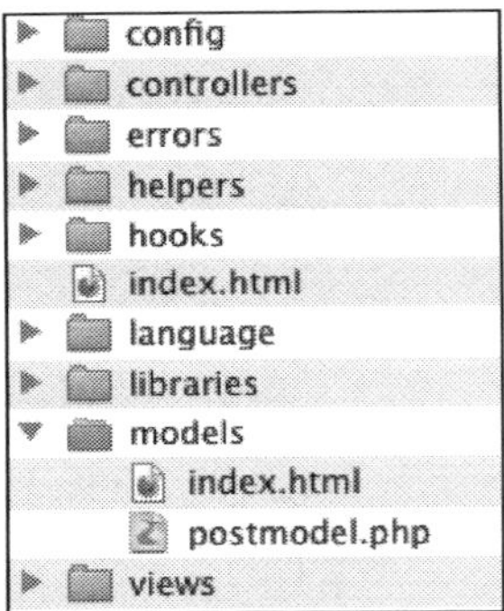

Finally, we'll use an extended Controller as well. Create a new Library file called `Rest_controller.php`.

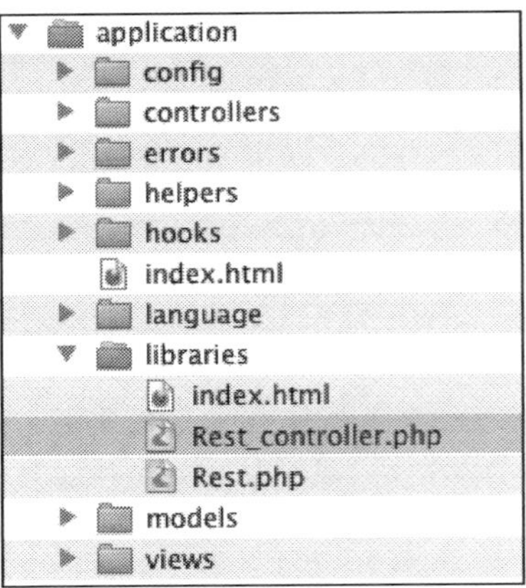

Setting up the database

Create a new database table and run the following SQL command on it to add our posts table:

```
CREATE TABLE `posts` (
`id` MEDIUMINT( 11 ) NOT NULL AUTO_INCREMENT PRIMARY KEY ,
`author` VARCHAR( 255 ) NOT NULL ,
`title` VARCHAR( 255 ) NOT NULL ,
`content` TEXT NOT NULL
) ENGINE = MYISAM ;
```

REST library

Because the library is the backbone of our REST Implementation, let's build out the functions now. We only have two functions in this Library. The `request()` function allows us to send a GET, POST, PUT or DELETE request easily. The `response()` function allows us to easily send back a response if an error occurs. We use `_format_xml()` and `_format_json()` to format the error if we send one using this library.

Base class

Here is the base to our class; this is where it all starts before we start fleshing the functions out.

```
<?php

class Rest
{
  var $CI;
  var $_formats = array(
          'xml'      => 'application/xml',
          'json'      => 'application/json'
);


  function request($url, $method = "GET", $data = NULL)
  {
    switch($method)
    {
      case "GET":

        break;
```

```
        case "PUT":

          break;

        case "POST":

          break;

        case "DELETE":

          break;

      }
    }

    function response($data, $http_status = 200, $format = 'xml')
    {

    }

    _format_xml($data)
    {

    }

    _format_json($data)
    {

    }
}
?>
```

Performing a GET request

To perform a GET request, we will be using cURL. The code that we use inititalises a curl session, we then set a few settings for cURL. Once we execute the cURL request and save it to a variable, we close the session, as we don't need it anymore. Finally, we send the `$data` variable to the `response()` function. This lets us easily get the response from the client.

```
case "GET":

  $ch = curl_init($url);
  curl_setopt($ch, CURLOPT_RETURNTRANSFER, true);
```

```
    curl_setopt($ch, CURLOPT_HEADER, 0);
    $data = curl_exec($ch);
    curl_close($ch);

    $this->CI->output->set_output($data);

    break;
```

Performing a PUT request

To perform a PUT request, we need to supply data to the function. The first thing that we do is to check if the `$data` variable is empty or not, and provide an error message if necessary. The next thing that we do is to format the array (all of the data that we send will be in an associative array) into the correct format to send across with the PUT request. The cURL code given next is the same sort of code as we discussed previously. The only difference is that we set some different settings—most notably the `CURLOPT_CUSTOMREQUEST`—this allows us to send a `PUT` request.

```
case "PUT":

if($data === NULL)
{
  $response =
    array('error' =>
      'You cannot perform a POST request with no data!');
  $this->response($response);
}
else
{
  $fields_string = "";

  foreach($data as $key=>$value)
    { $fields_string .= $key.'='.$value.'&'; }
  rtrim($fields_string,'&');

  $ch = curl_init($url);
  curl_setopt($ch, CURLOPT_RETURNTRANSFER, true);
  curl_setopt($ch,CURLOPT_CUSTOMREQUEST, "PUT");
  curl_setopt($ch,CURLOPT_POSTFIELDS,$fields_string);
  $data = curl_exec($ch);
  curl_close($ch);

  echo($data);
}

break;
```

Performing a POST request

Performing a `POST` request is almost identical to performing a `PUT` request, the difference being that we don't send a custom request parameter. Take a look at the following code:

```
case "POST":

if($data === NULL)
{
    $response = "You cannot perform a POST request with no data!";
    $this->response($response);
}
else
{
    $fields_string = "";

    foreach($data as $key=>$value)
      { $fields_string .= $key.'='.$value.'&'; }
    rtrim($fields_string,'&');


    $ch = curl_init($url);
    curl_setopt($ch, CURLOPT_RETURNTRANSFER, true);
    curl_setopt($ch,CURLOPT_POST,count($data));
    curl_setopt($ch,CURLOPT_POSTFIELDS,$fields_string);
    $data = curl_exec($ch);
    curl_close($ch);

    echo($data);
}

break;
```

Performing a DELETE request

Performing a `DELETE` request, again using cURL, is very simple. Just as for performing a `PUT` request, we set the `CURLOPT_CUSTOMREQUEST` option. The rest of the code is the same as the previous functions.

```
case "DELETE":

$ch = curl_init($url);
curl_setopt($ch, CURLOPT_RETURNTRANSFER, true);
curl_setopt($ch,CURLOPT_CUSTOMREQUEST, "DELETE");
```

```
    curl_setopt($ch, CURLOPT_HEADER, 0);
    $data = curl_exec($ch);
    curl_close($ch);

    echo($data);

    break;
```

Response function

Now we need to create the response function. We use this to return any errors to the client. We need to use a function for this so we can format the response as either XML or JSON.

```
function response($data, $http_status = 200, $format = 'xml')
  {
    if(empty($data))
      {
        $this->output->set_status_header(404);
        return;
      }

      $this->output->set_status_header($http_status);

        if(method_exists($this, '_format_'.$format))
        {
        $this->output->
          set_header('Content-type: ' . $this->_formats[$format]);

          $final_data = $this->{'_format_'.$format}($data);
          $this->output->set_output($final_data);
        }
        else
    {
          $this->output->set_output($data);
        }
  }
```

In this function we take the data, an HTTP response code, and the format type that we wish to use to format the data. If the data is empty we set the status header as 404 and return; otherwise we set the header as whatever header was passed to the function, or default to 200 OK. If the format method exists, then we set the content header, pass the data to the format function and pass the formatted data to the output buffer. If the format method requested does not exist, we simply return the data.

The format XML function

This function is used to take an array and format it into XML. This function uses the XMLWriter class in PHP and uses it to format the data to XML. The first few lines set up an XMLWriter object, set what version of XML we want to return, and set a root element. Next we have a function inside this function. We use this function so that if we have arrays contained within our array we can call this function from within the function. We could recursively call `_format_xml()`, but then we'd end up with another XML opening tag. The write function simply takes the `$xml` object and the `$data` array and adds it to the XML object, which in turn is turned into XML.

```
function _format_xml($data)
{
  $xml = new XmlWriter();
  $xml->openMemory();
  $xml->startDocument('1.0', 'UTF-8');
  $xml->startElement('root');

  function write(XMLWriter $xml, $data)
  {
    foreach($data as $key => $value)
    {
      if(is_array($value))
      {
        if(is_numeric($key))
        {
          $key = 'id';
        }
        $xml->startElement($key);
        write($xml, $value);
        $xml->endElement();
        continue;
      }
      $xml->writeElement($key, $value);
    }
  }
  write($xml, $data);

  $xml->endElement();
  echo $xml->outputMemory(true);
}
```

The format JSON function

The format JSON function is used for the same purpose as the format XML function. This function is much simpler, though—we simply call `json_encode()` and pass the array to it.

```
function _format_json($data)
{
  return json_encode($data);
}
```

Final library code

Here is our final library code, for clarification:

```
<?php

class Rest
{
  var $CI;
  var $_formats = array(
          'xml'     => 'application/xml',
          'json'     => 'application/json'
          );

  function Rest()
  {
    $this->CI =& get_instance();
  }

  function request($url, $method = "GET", $data = NULL)
  {
    if($url === NULL) { $url = $this->server . $this->uri; }

    switch($method)
    {
      case "GET":
        $ch = curl_init($url);
        curl_setopt($ch, CURLOPT_RETURNTRANSFER, true);
        curl_setopt($ch, CURLOPT_HEADER, 0);
        $data = curl_exec($ch);
        curl_close($ch);

        echo($data);
```

```
    break;

  case "PUT":

    if($data === NULL)
    {
      $response = array('error' =>
        'You cannot perform a POST request with no data!');
      $this->response($response);
    }
    else
    {
      $fields_string = "";

      foreach($data as $key=>$value)
        { $fields_string .= $key.'='.$value.'&'; }
      rtrim($fields_string,'&');

      $ch = curl_init($url);
      curl_setopt($ch, CURLOPT_RETURNTRANSFER, true);
      curl_setopt($ch,CURLOPT_CUSTOMREQUEST, "PUT");
      curl_setopt($ch,CURLOPT_POSTFIELDS,$fields_string);
      $data = curl_exec($ch);
      curl_close($ch);

      echo($data);
    }

    break;

  case "POST":

    if($data === NULL)
    {
      $response =
        "You cannot perform a POST request with no data!";
      $this->response($response);
    }
    else
    {
      $fields_string = "";

      foreach($data as $key=>$value)
        { $fields_string .= $key.'='.$value.'&'; }
```

```
        rtrim($fields_string,'&');


        $ch = curl_init($url);
        curl_setopt($ch, CURLOPT_RETURNTRANSFER, true);
        curl_setopt($ch,CURLOPT_POST,count($data));
        curl_setopt($ch,CURLOPT_POSTFIELDS,$fields_string);
        $data = curl_exec($ch);
        curl_close($ch);

        echo($data);
      }

      break;

    case "DELETE":

      $ch = curl_init($url);
      curl_setopt($ch, CURLOPT_RETURNTRANSFER, true);
      curl_setopt($ch,CURLOPT_CUSTOMREQUEST, "DELETE");
      curl_setopt($ch, CURLOPT_HEADER, 0);
      $data = curl_exec($ch);
      curl_close($ch);

      echo($data);

      break;
  }
}

function response($data, $http_status = 200, $format = 'xml')
{
  if(empty($data))
    {
      $this->output->set_status_header(404);
      return;
    }

    $this->output->set_status_header($http_status);

      if(method_exists($this, '_format_'.$format))
      {
      $this->output->
        set_header('Content-type: ' . $this->_formats[$format]);
```

```
            $final_data = $this->{'_format_'.$format}($data);
            $this->output->set_output($final_data);
          }
          else
      {
            $this->output->set_output($data);
          }
    }


    function _format_xml($data)
  {
    $xml = new XmlWriter();
    $xml->openMemory();
    $xml->startDocument('1.0', 'UTF-8');
    $xml->startElement('root');

    function write(XMLWriter $xml, $data)
    {
      foreach($data as $key => $value)
      {
        if(is_array($value))
        {
          if(is_numeric($key))
          {
            $key = 'id';
          }
          $xml->startElement($key);
          write($xml, $value);
          $xml->endElement();
          continue;
        }
        $xml->writeElement($key, $value);
      }
    }
    write($xml, $data);

    $xml->endElement();
    echo $xml->outputMemory(true);
  }

    function _format_json($data)
    {
```

```
        return json_encode($data);
      }
    }

    ?>
```

Rest Controller

The Rest Controller that we will use is an extended Controller with all of our Rest functionality inside of it. You'll learn all about extended Controllers in the next chapter.

Base class

This is the Base to our class. The only thing that we'll go over is the `_remap()` function. We've seen the other functions before, as we're just placing the response functions in this Controller.

```
<?php

class Rest_controller extends Controller
{

  var $request_method;
  var $id;
  var $method;
  var $_formats = array(
              'xml'      => 'application/xml',
              'json'      => 'application/json'
  );

  function Rest_controller()
  {
    parent::Controller();
    $this->request_method = $_SERVER['REQUEST_METHOD'];
    $this->id = (int) $this->uri->segment("3");
    $this->method = $this->uri->segment("2");
  }

  function _remap()
  {
    if($this->method != "index")
    {
      if($this->id == NULL)
      {
```

```
        switch($this->request_method)
        {
          case "GET":

            break;

          case "POST":

            break;

          case "DELETE":

            break;
        }
      }
      else
      {
        switch($this->request_method)
        {

          case "GET":

            break;

          case "PUT":

            break;

          case "DELETE":

            break;
        }
      }
    }
    else
    {

    }
  }

  function response($data, $http_status = 200, $format = 'xml') { }

  function _format_xml($data) { }
```

```
    function _format_json($data) { }
}

?>
```

The _remap() function

The `_remap()` function is used to remap the REST requests from the usual CodeIgniter URI to another function, depending on the type of request. If we have a GET request to the posts function, the function we'll remap to will be `post_get()`, which is the name of the requested function with the request method appended to the end. The `_remap()` function also checks to see whether or not an ID was given. If one was, it limits the types of requests, and passes the ID to the function.

```
function _remap()
{
  if($this->method != "index")
  {
    if($this->id == NULL)
    {
      switch($this->request_method)
      {
        case "GET":
          $this->{$this->method . "_get"}();
          break;

        case "POST":
          $this->{$this->method . "_post"}();
          break;

        case "DELETE":
          $this->{$this->method . "_delete"}();
          break;
      }
    }
    else
    {
      switch($this->request_method)
      {

        case "GET":
          $this->{$this->method . "_get"}($this->id);
          break;
```

```
            case "PUT":
              $this->{$this->method . "_put"}($this->id);
              break;

            case "DELETE":
              $this->{$this->method . "_delete"}($this->id);
              break;
          }
        }
      }
      else
      {
        $this->index();
      }
    }
```

Server Controller

The Server Controller is our gateway to the data in the database. This is the Controller that we will be performing all of our requests on in order to get, create, update, and delete data.

Base class

Here is the our base class before we start building it all out:

```
<?php

include(APPPATH . "libraries/Rest_controller.php");

class Server extends Rest_controller
{

  function Server()
  {
    parent::Rest_controller();
    $this->load->database();
  }

  function post_get($id = NULL)
  {
    if($id == NULL)
    {
```

```
        }
        else
        {

        }
    }

    function post_put($id)
    {

    }

    function post_post()
    {

    }

    function post_delete($id = NULL)
    {

    }
}

?>
```

As you can see, we have four different functions. `post_get()` handles all of the `GET` requests; `post_put()` handles all of the PUT requests; `post_post()` handles all of the POST requests; and `post_delete()` handles all of the DELETE requests.

The post_get() function

The first function that we will be coding is when a `GET` request has been made.

```
function post_get($id = NULL)
{
  if($id == NULL)
  {
    $data = $this->postmodel->get_post();
    $this->response($data);
  }
  else
  {
    $data = $this->postmodel->get_post($id);
    $this->response($data);
  }
}
```

The first thing that we do is to check whether or not an ID has been passed in. If there is no ID, then we simply call the model function `get_post()` and pass the data to the response function that is contained in the rest controller. If there is an ID, then we do exactly the same thing but we pass the ID to the model function so that it can limit the result to the correct ID.

The post_put() function

Because a PUT request is basically how we edit blog posts, we should always provide an ID. In this function, if there is no ID then a PHP error will occur.

```
function post_put($id)
{
  // get the put data from the input stream
  parse_str(file_get_contents("php://input"), $put_data);
  $this->postmodel->update_post($put_data, $id);

  $message = array('id' => $id, 'message' => 'Edited!');
  $this->response($message);
}
```

Instead of running a model function to get the data, this time we get the contents from the PHP input stream. By running the input stream through `parse_str()`, we eliminate the need to parse the stream ourselves. We store the array in `$put_data`, and run this through the model function in order to update the post, along with the ID of the post that we want to edit. We set a response as an array with the ID and the message "Edited!"

The post_delete() function

This is how we delete items from the database.

```
function post_delete($id = NULL)
{
  if($id == NULL)
  {
    $this->postmodel->delete_post();

    $message = array('message' => 'Deleted!');
    $this->response($message);
  }
  else
  {
    $this->postmodel->delete_post($id);
```

```
        $message = array('message' => 'Deleted!');
        $this->response($message);
      }
    }
```

This is much the same as performing a GET request. We check to see if an ID has been passed or not; if not, then we know to delete all of the posts, so we run the model function delete_post() and it will delete all of the posts. If an ID has been supplied then we do the same thing, but pass in the ID to the model function so it knows to only delete one record.

The post_post() function

This function allows us to add a new blog post. We won't need an ID as this function creates a new record with a new ID, so there is no need to check if an ID has been passed.

```
function post_post()
{
  $this->postmodel->create_post($_POST);

  $message = array('message' => 'Added!');
  $this->response($message);
}
```

We simply call a model function and pass the $_POST global variable to it. We set a success message and return it as a response.

Final server controller code

As always, here's the full server controller code:

```
<?php

include(APPPATH . "libraries/Rest_controller.php");

class Server extends Rest_controller
{

  function Server()
  {
    parent::Rest_controller();
    $this->load->database();
  }
```

```
function post_get($id = NULL)
{
  if($id == NULL)
  {
    $data = $this->postmodel->get_post();
    $this->response($data);
  }
  else
  {
    $data = $this->postmodel->get_post($id);
    $this->response($data);
  }
}

function post_put($id)
{
  // get the put data from the input stream
  parse_str(file_get_contents("php://input"), $put_data);
  $this->postmodel->update_post($put_data, $id);

  $message = array('id' => $id, 'message' => 'Edited!');
  $this->response($message);
}

function post_post()
{
  $this->postmodel->create_post($_POST);

  $message = array('message' => 'Added!');
  $this->response($message);
}

function post_delete($id = NULL)
{
  if($id == NULL)
  {
    $this->postmodel->delete_post();

    $message = array('message' => 'Deleted!');
    $this->response($message);
  }
  else
  {
    $this->postmodel->delete_post($id);
```

```
            $message = array('message' => 'Deleted!');
            $this->response($message);
        }
    }

}

?>
```

Post Model

The last piece of our REST Web Service puzzle is our Post Model. So far we haven't built any of the model, we only have an empty file.

Base class

Here is our Base class. We simply create out functions and the general structure of them. The functions that have an optional ID parameter check to see if the ID variable is NULL and will perform the appropriate action depending on the result.

```
<?php

class Postmodel extends Model
{

  function Postmodel()
  {
    parent::Model();
    $this->load->database();
  }

  function get_post($id = NULL)
  {
    if($id === NULL)
    {

    }
    else
    {

    }
  }

  function update_post($data, $id)
```

```
    {

    }

    function create_post($data)
    {

    }

    function delete_post($id = NULL)
    {
      if($id === NULL)
      {

      }
      else
      {

      }
    }

}

?>
```

The get_post() function

The get post function is used to retrieve either a single blog post or all of the blog posts.

```
function get_post($id = NULL)
{
  if($id === NULL)
  {
    $query = $this->db->get('posts');
    $result = $query->result_array();

    return $result;
  }
  else
  {
    $id = (int) $id;

    $this->db->where('id', $id);
```

```
        $query = $this->db->get('posts');
        $result = $query->row_array();

        return $result;
    }
}
```

The first thing that we do is to check the ID variable's value. If it is NULL then we know that the request is for all of the blog posts. We perform the query by using the CodeIgniter Active Record Library, grab the result and return it from the function.

If the ID variable has a value other than NULL, then we typecast the variable to an Integer in order to avoid any SQL Errors. Then we set the `WHERE` clause of our query by using the Active Record Library, and then perform the query the same as before. This time though, instead of returning the `result_array()` we return the `row_array()` — this will only return a single row, because that's all we need, and this is the best way to generate the result. Then we finally return the resulting variable.

The update_post() function

The update post function can only work with data passed into it along with an ID.

```
function update_post($data, $id)
{
  $id = (int) $id;
  $items = array();

  if(array_key_exists('author', $data))
    { $items['author'] = $data['author']; } else { return FALSE; }
  if(array_key_exists('title', $data))
    { $items['title'] = $data['title']; } else { return FALSE; }
  if(array_key_exists('content', $data))
    { $items['content'] = $data['content']; } else { return FALSE; }

  $this->db->where('id', $id);
  $this->db->update('posts', $items);
}
```

The first thing that we do is to typecast the ID variable to ensure that it is an Integer. We also create a variable to put the array items into. We create a new array so that anyone trying to insert anything into the database that isn't expected can't do it. We only add the expected array items into this final "clean" array.

Once this is done, we check the array to see if the three array keys exist: author, title, and content. If either of these keys is missing from the array then we simply return `FALSE`. If everything works fine, however, we set the `WHERE` clause of the query and update the database by using the Active Record Class.

The create_post() function

The create post function can only be used in one way, unlike the get post function. This function is much like the function that was explained previously, with some minor differences, such as no ID being given, and we use the `insert()` function instead of the `update()` function of the Active Record Class.

```
function create_post($data)
{
  $items = array();

  if(array_key_exists('author', $data))
    { $items['author'] = $data['author']; } else { return FALSE; }
  if(array_key_exists('title', $data))
    { $items['title'] = $data['title']; } else { return FALSE; }
  if(array_key_exists('content', $data))
    { $items['content'] = $data['content']; } else { return FALSE; }

  $this->db->insert('posts', $items);
}
```

The delete_post() function

The delete post functions works in the same way as the get post function.

```
function delete_post($id = NULL)
{
  if($id === NULL)
  {
    $this->db->empty_table('posts');
  }
  else
  {
    $id = (int) $id;
    $this->db->where('id', $id);
    $this->db->delete('posts');
  }
}
```

Firstly, we check to see if the ID variable is NULL. If it is, we simply empty the table because the ID of a specific post wasn't specified. If the ID variable is not NULL we typecast it to an Integer, to avoid any errors and perform the query just like we have always done.

Final post model code

Here is the final post model code:

```
<?php

class Postmodel extends Model
{

  function Postmodel()
  {
    parent::Model();
    $this->load->database();
  }

  function get_post($id = NULL)
  {
    if($id === NULL)
    {
      $query = $this->db->get('posts');
      $result = $query->result_array();

      return $result;
    }
    else
    {
      $this->db->where('id', $id);
      $query = $this->db->get('posts');
      $result = $query->row_array();

      return $result;
    }
  }

  function update_post($data, $id)
  {
    $id = (int) $id;
    $items = array();

    if(array_key_exists('author', $data))
```

```
    { $items['author'] = $data['author']; } else { return FALSE; }
  if(array_key_exists('title', $data))
    { $items['title'] = $data['title']; } else { return FALSE; }
  if(array_key_exists('content', $data))
   { $items['content'] = $data['content']; } else { return FALSE; }

  $this->db->where('id', $id);
  $this->db->update('posts', $items);
}

function create_post($data)
{
  $items = array();

  if(array_key_exists('author', $data))
    { $items['author'] = $data['author']; } else { return FALSE; }
  if(array_key_exists('title', $data))
    { $items['title'] = $data['title']; } else { return FALSE; }
  if(array_key_exists('content', $data))
   { $items['content'] = $data['content']; } else { return FALSE; }

  $this->db->insert('posts', $items);
}

function delete_post($id = NULL)
{
  if($id === NULL)
  {
    $this->db->empty_table('posts');
  }
  else
  {
    $id = (int) $id;
    $this->db->where('id', $id);
    $this->db->delete('posts');
  }
}

}

?>
```

Create a new post

To create a new post, all we need to do is perform a new POST request to the URL of the Post Controller (or server if we were doing this on a real project). We also need to send the new blog post across. We do this by creating a new serialized array with three keys: author, title, and content. Then we simply fill the array keys with the blog post author, post title and the post content, and we're all set.

Take special care when going over the line of code where we perform the request. The first parameter is the URL of the server. The second parameter is the type of request that we want to make. This is optional and defaults to GET. The final parameter is the data that you want to send across the request. This is also optional.

```
<?php

class Client extends Controller
{

  function Client()
  {
    parent::Controller();
    $this->load->library('rest');
  }

  function index()
  {
    $data = array(
        'author' => 'blog post author',
        'title' => 'blog post title',
        'content' => 'blog post content'
      );

    $request = $this->rest->
      request("http://localhost/0905_08/index.php/server/post/",
        "POST", $data);

  }

}

?>
```

Update a post

Updating a post is essentially exactly the same as creating a new post. The only difference is that the URL that you perform the request on will contain an ID in the third URI string segment, and the request type will be `PUT` and not `POST`. Take a look at the next example. The ID that you put in the third URI string segment should be the same as the ID stored inside the database.

```
<?php

class Client extends Controller
{

  function Client()
  {
    parent::Controller();
    $this->load->library('rest');
  }

  function index()
  {
    $data = array(
        'author' => 'blog post author new',
        'title' => 'blog post title new',
        'content' => 'blog post content new'
      );

    $request = $this->rest->
      request("http://localhost/0905_08/index.php/server/post/index/4",
        "PUT", $data);

  }

}

?>
```

Delete a post

Deleting a blog post is very easy. We change the request method from either of the two previous examples from `POST` or `PUT` to `DELETE`. We can remove the serialized array from the code altogether, as in this case it isn't needed. Then we select our URL carefully. If we want to delete a single post, we supply a URL with an ID appended to the third URI string segment, as seen in the next example:

```
<?php

class Client extends Controller
{

  function Client()
  {
    parent::Controller();
    $this->load->library('rest');
  }

  function index()
  {
    $request = $this->rest->
     request("http://localhost/0905_08/index.php/server/post/4/",
             "DELETE");

  }

}

?>
```

If we wanted to delete all of the blog posts, however, we simply remove the ID from the URL altogether.

```
<?php

class Client extends Controller
{

  function Client()
  {
    parent::Controller();
    $this->load->library('rest');
  }
```

```
  function index()
  {
    $request = $this->rest->
      request("http://localhost/0905_08/index.php/server/post",
              "DELETE");

  }

}

?>
```

Get a blog post

Just like deleting a blog post, we can get either a single blog post or all of the posts. It works in pretty much the same way as deleting a blog post. If we want all of the posts we simply perform a `GET` request using the REST Library on the server URL. If we only want a single blog post we add the ID to the third URI string segment. Here are two examples of this. The first example shows how we would get all blog posts, whilst the second shows how we would get a single post. Remember that we don't need to explicitly set the request method to `GET`, as this is the default.

```
<?php

class Client extends Controller
{

  function Client()
  {
    parent::Controller();
    $this->load->library('rest');
  }

  function index()
  {
    $request = $this->rest->
      request("http://localhost/0905_08/index.php/server/post/");

  }

}

?>
```

```
<?php

class Client extends Controller
{

  function Client()
  {
    parent::Controller();
    $this->load->library('rest');
  }

  function index()
  {
    $request = $this->rest->
     request("http://localhost/0905_08/index.php/server/post/4");

  }

}

?>
```

Summary

There we have it. We have now built ourselves a fully working REST Web Service. Although this implementation is currently at a basic level, we could expand it more to include authentication and a more rigid way of determining the request method, making it even easier for us to create web services. Now that we know how REST works, we are all able to implement this in more of our projects, helping us to create projects even faster than before by utilizing other web services instead of reinventing the wheel.

9
Extending CodeIgniter

CodeIgniter is an awesome PHP Framework, but it doesn't have everything that anyone could ever need in the core. Instead, it allows us to extend pretty much every aspect of the framework. We can extend the core libraries to include additional features, or overwrite them completely. We can create extended Controller and Model classes to include extra functionality for different types of pages and features. If we simply want to add a few functions to the framework, we can create helpers to simply add these few functions into our arsenal. At the other end of the scale, if we want to change the way that CodeIgniter works, or want to run a script mid way through the application flow, then we can create a hook to do this for us, without having to hack the core files, which could potentially screw up our installation when we come to upgrade.

In this chapter we will:

- Learn about hooks, and build a very simple hook into our CodeIgniter installation
- Learn about extended Controllers and why you would need them, with examples
- Build our own custom User Authentication Library
- Extend the CodeIgniter Session Library to use native PHP sessions
- Build a helper to make some of our user authentication jobs easier
- Learn about some of the hidden gems in CodeIgniter

Hooks

Hooks are a way to change the way that CodeIgniter runs without actually hacking any of the core files. Hooks allow you to run a function at eight different points in the system execution.

Hook points

pre_system

This hook point is called very early during system execution. Only the benchmark and hooks class have been loaded at this point.

pre_controller

This is called immediately before your Controller is called. All other classes have been loaded by this point.

post_controller_constructor

Called immediately after your Controller has been instantiated, but prior to any method calls being made.

post_controller

Called immediately after your Controller is executed.

display_override

This overrides the `_display()` function, which is used to send the page to the browser after execution. This lets you use your own display methodology. You will need to access the CodeIgniter Super Object by using `$this->CI =& get_instance()` and finalize the data by using `$this->CI->output->get_output()`.

cache_override

This allows you to use your own `_display_cache()` function from the output class.

scaffolding_override

This lets a scaffolding request trigger your script.

post_system

This is run after the page has been delivered to the browser, which happens after the system has gone through full execution and the finalized data has been sent to the browser. This is great for hooks that log data, such as user data (where a user has been on the website) as it is called after everything has been sent to the browser, so you know it will not effect how the website looks.

Our hook

We will create a very simple hook. We will create a hook to define whether or not our site is on maintenance. We'll simply set a variable and show an error if we should be on maintenance.

Enable hooks

Before we can use hooks we need to enable them. Open up your `config.php` file and find the following line:

```
$config['enable_hooks'] = FALSE;
```

Change it to:

```
$config['enable_hooks'] = TRUE;
```

Define a hook

Open up `config/hooks.php` and enter the following code into it. This will ensure that our hook is loaded.

```
$hook['pre_controller'] = array(
                                'class'    => 'Maintenance',
                                'function' => 'decide',
                                'filename' => 'maintenance.php',
                                'filepath' => 'hooks',
                                'params' => 'FALSE'
                                );
```

This sets the class, function, filename, and filepath to our hooks file. We also send a single parameter, which will be passed to the function `decide()`. This hook will be called before the system has executed. This is because if we are on a maintenance break, we don't need to load all of the CodeIgniter Libraries, routing functions, and so on. To put the system offline, simply change the `params` to `TRUE`, and change it back to `FALSE` to put it back online again.

Our hook

Create a new file inside the `application/hooks/` folder, called `Maintenance.php`. The following code is the content of our file:

```
<?php

class Maintenance
{
```

```
    function decide($maintenance)
    {
      if($maintenance == TRUE)
      {
        show_error('The system is offline for maintenance.');
      }
    }
  }

  ?>
```

This file is very simple. If the parameter sent to the function is `TRUE` then we show an error that the site is offline for maintenance. If not, we don't do anything. This is a very simple example of a hook, but shows how they work very well.

Extended controllers

Extended Controllers can be extremely helpful when building CodeIgniter applications. You might find, when developing different applications with CodeIgniter, that some of your Controllers have overlapping functionality. Instead of recreating the functions each time, you can make use of an extended Controller class.

Essentially what you do is create a new file in the libraries folder called `MY_Controller.php`—simply create this Controller like you would any other Controller. This file will be called by the system automatically.

If you want to have a number of extending Controllers, however, you may want to use a different name for your files.

> I have given these controllers a suffix of `_controller` so that I can easily identify them as a Controller file and not a general purpose library. You may use any type of naming convention that you please as long as it works for you. I simply do it this way because I find it easy and it helps me work better.

Admin controller

When building a web application with CodeIgniter, you may find yourself repeating code for an administration panel—such as checking that users are logged in before being allowed access to the admin panel.

To do this, simply create a new file inside `system/application/libraries/` called `admin_controller.php`.

This will build on the User Authentication system that we created in *Chapter 5, User Authentication 2*. We'll check that the user is logged in before sending them to the admin panel or displaying an error message.

Copy the following code into this newly-created file:

```
<?php

class admin_controller extends Controller
{

  function admin_controller()
  {
    parent::Controller();

    $this->load->model('account_model');

    if($this->account_model->logged_in() === FALSE)
    {
      show_error("You must be logged in to view this page.");
    }
  }

}

?>
```

To use this Controller instead of the usual base Controller class, simply require the admin Controller file as shown next, and extend `admin_controller` instead of `Controller`. If your Controller has a constructor, you should also run the admin constructor as follows: `parent::admin_controller();` so that we can have access to the CodeIgniter objects.

The Admin Controller is very basic. All we do is load the account model from *Chapter 5, User Authentication 2*, and check to see if the user is logged in. If so, we display an error message. We do it this way around because when the function `show_error()` is used it will only display the error message, and will omit any of the page that may have been loaded.

Extending Controllers is a great way to add new functionality to Controllers without hacking the core or repeating yourself unnecessarily. This method will also work for Models and Libraries. For example, you could create an extended Model with basic CRUD functions built in.

Extended libraries

We are going to extend the Session library to use native PHP sessions instead of being cookie based.

Before we start to create the library, we need to know how to extend libraries. All CodeIgniter classes are prefixed with `CI_` - and all our extended classes should be prefixed with `MY_` - this is configurable, just open up your `config.php` file and edit the following line:

```
$config['subclass_prefix'] = 'MY_';
```

Our filename needs to be `MY_Session.php` (or whatever you set your prefix to be) and the class will be `MY_Session` and it will extend `CI_Session`. When loading the class, though, we don't need to use the prefix; we simply use `session` and CodeIgniter will load the extended class for us.

We could completely replace the class by leaving out the `extends` clause on our class declaration—but we don't want to do that as we don't want to overwrite the flash data functionality. This library will work in exactly the same way as the CodeIgniter Session Class: we don't change the way we use it, only the way it stores information.

The library

Go ahead and create a new library file inside the `/system/application/libraries/` folder, called `MY_Session.php`.

The functions that we'll be building are: `set_userdata()`, `unset_userdata()`, `userdata()`, and `sess_destroy()`.

Base class

Here is the base of our class; we simply create the functions that we'll be using. We have built the function `sess_destroy()` because this is only a wrapper function for a native PHP function.

```
<?php
session_start();

class MY_Session extends CI_Session
{
  function MY_Session()
  {
    parent::CI_Session();
  }

  function userdata($item)
  {

  }

  function set_userdata($items, $value = NULL)
  {

  }

  function unset_userdata($items)
  {

  }

  function sess_destroy()
  {
    session_destroy();
  }
}

?>
```

userdata()

This function takes an item key and checks that it exists in the session variable; if it does, then we return it; if not we return FALSE.

```
function userdata($item)
{
  if(empty($_SESSION[$item]))
  {
    return FALSE;
  }
  else
  {
    return $_SESSION[$item];
  }
}
```

set_userdata()

This function creates user data. We can set data by using an associative array or by passing the item key to the first function and the value to the second. Because we can accept two types of input, we have to check if the first variable is an array. If it is then we simply run through it and set all of the items. If it isn't, we just set the first, and use the second variable to get the value.

```
function set_userdata($items, $value = NULL)
{
  if(is_array($items))
  {
    foreach($items as $item => $value)
    {
      $_SESSION[$item] = $value;
    }
  }
  else
  {
    $_SESSION[$items] = $value;
  }
}
```

unset_userdata()

This function works identically to the previous one, except that we don't need a second parameter, and instead of setting the data, we use `unset()` to remove it.

```
function unset_userdata($items)
{
  if(is_array($items))
  {
    foreach($items as $item => $value)
    {
      unset($_SESSION[$item]);
    }
  }
  else
  {
    unset($_SESSION[$items]);
  }
}
```

Full library code

Here is the full library code, for clarity:

```
<?php
session_start();

class MY_Session extends CI_Session
{
  function MY_Session()
  {
    parent::CI_Session();
  }

  function userdata($item)
  {
    if(empty($_SESSION[$item]))
    {
      return FALSE;
    }
    else
    {
      return $_SESSION[$item];
    }
```

```
    }

    function set_userdata($items, $value = NULL)
    {
      if(is_array($items))
      {
        foreach($items as $item => $value)
        {
          $_SESSION[$item] = $value;
        }
      }
      else
      {
        $_SESSION[$items] = $value;
      }
    }

    function unset_userdata($items)
    {
      if(is_array($items))
      {
        foreach($items as $item => $value)
        {
          unset($_SESSION[$item]);
        }
      }
      else
      {
        unset($_SESSION[$items]);
      }
    }

    function sess_destroy()
    {
      session_destroy();
    }
  }

  ?>
```

Custom libraries

Just as we can extend the native CodeIgniter Libraries, we can also create entirely new libraries and use them just as seamlessly as native libraries. We'll take our Account Model from earlier in the book and create a library out of it, and then add some extra features.

The features

The Authentication library will have the basic functions you would expect:

- Login
- Logout
- Register

We'll leave the form validation stuff in our Controller, as we've already built that. We could contain all of the functionality, including the form views and form validation, in the library as I have done with my own open-source authentication library, but that seems like overkill—especially for the book format.

The library

The first thing to do is to create our Library file. Create a new file inside the `/system/application/libraries/` folder, called `Auth.php`.

```
<?php

class Auth
{

  var $CI;

  function Account_model()
  {
    parent::Model();
    $this->CI->load->database();
    $this->CI->load->library('session');
  }

  function create($data)
  {
    if($this->CI->db->insert('users', $data))
    {
```

```
            return TRUE;
          }
          else
          {
            return FALSE;
          }
        }

        function login()
        {
          $data = array(
                         'username' => $this->CI->input->post('username'),
                         'logged_in' => TRUE
                         );

          $this->CI->session->set_userdata($data);
        }

        function logged_in()
        {
          if($this->CI->session->userdata('logged_in') == TRUE)
          {
            return TRUE;
          }
          else
          {
            return FALSE;
          }
        }

        function logout()
        {
          $this->CI->session->sess_destroy();
        }
      }

      ?>
```

This is essentially the same as our Model, except we have added a logout function. The whole point of creating this library is that we can easily extend the functionality of it, for example by adding group functions and a restricting function to groups. If we added these types of functions to a Model, we'd be breaking MVC, as the Model is a data abstraction layer. This library helps us to keep everything in one file.

The controller

We need to make a few changes to our Controller. We need to use the functions in the library instead of the Model. Here is the code, with the changes:

```
<?php

class Account extends Controller
{
  function Account()
  {
    parent::Controller();

    // Load the resources needed for the Controller
    $this->load->library('auth');
    $this->load->helper(array('url', 'form'));
    $this->load->model('account_model');

    $this->_salt = "123456789987654321";
  }

  function index()
  {
    if($this->auth->logged_in() === TRUE)
    {
      $this->dashboard(TRUE);
    }
    else
    {
      $this->load->view('account/details');
    }
  }

  function dashboard($condition = FALSE)
  {
    if($condition === TRUE OR $this->auth->logged_in() === TRUE)
    {
      $this->load->view('account/dashboard');
    }
    else
    {
      $this->load->view('account/details');
    }
  }
```

```
function login()
{
  // Set the form validation rules
  $this->form_validation->
    set_rules('username', 'Username',
      'xss_clean|required|callback_username_check');
  $this->form_validation->
    set_rules('password', 'Password',
      'xss_clean|required|min_length[4]|max_length[12]|
        callback_password_check');

  // Set the username and password as class variables so
  // we can use them in the callbacks
  $this->_username = $this->input->post('username');
  $this->_password =
    sha1($this->_salt . $this->input->post('password'));
      // hash and salt the password

  if($this->form_validation->run() == FALSE)
  {
    $this->load->view('account/login');
  }
  else
  {
    $this->auth->login();

    $data['message'] =
      "You are logged in! Now go take a look at the "
          . anchor('account/dashboard', 'Dashboard');
    $this->load->view('account/success', $data);
  }
}

function register()
{
  // Set the form validation rules
  $this->form_validation->
    set_rules('username', 'Username', 'xss_clean|required');
  $this->form_validation->
    set_rules('email', 'Email Address',
      'xss_clean|required|valid_email|callback_email_exists');
  $this->form_validation->
    set_rules('password', 'Password',
      'xss_clean|required|min_length[4]|max_length[12]|
```

```
            matches[password_conf]|sha1');

    $this->form_validation->
      set_rules('password_conf', 'Password Confirmation',
        'xss_clean|required|matches[password]');

    if($this->form_validation->run() == FALSE)
    {
      $this->load->view('account/register');
    }
    else
    {
      $data['username'] = $this->input->post('username');
      $data['email'] = $this->input->post('email');
      $data['password'] =
        sha1($this->_salt . $this->input->post('password'));

      if($this->auth->create($data) === TRUE)
      {
        $data['message'] =
          "The user account has now been created! You can login " .
            anchor('account/login', 'here') . ".";
        $this->load->view('account/success', $data);
      }
      else
      {
        $data['error'] =
    "There was a problem when adding your account to the database.";
        $this->load->view('account/error', $data);
      }
    }
  }

  function logout()
  {
    $this->session->sess_destroy();
    $this->load->view('account/logout');
  }

  function password_check()
  {
    $query = $this->db->get_where('users',
      array('username' => $this->_username,
            'password' => $this->_password));
```

```
      if($query->num_rows() == 0)
      {
        $this->form_validation->
          set_message('username_check', 'There was an error!');
        return FALSE;
      }

      $query->free_result();

      return TRUE;
    }

    function user_exists($user)
    {
      $query = $this->db->
        get_where('users', array('username' => $user));

      if($query->num_rows() > 0)
      {
        $this->form_validation->
          set_message('user_exists',
            'The %s already exists in our database, please use a
different one.');
        return FALSE;
      }

      $query->free_result();

      return TRUE;
    }

    function email_exists($email)
    {
      $query = $this->db->get_where('users', array('email' => $email));

      if($query->num_rows() > 0)
      {
        $this->form_validation->
          set_message('email_exists',
            'The %s already exists in our database, please use a
different one.');
        return FALSE;
      }
```

```
        $query->free_result();

        return TRUE;
    }

}

?>
```

Helpers

We'll be creating a helper file to make it easier (and quicker) to see if a user is logged in or not. First, create a file inside the /system/application/helpers/ folder, called auth.php. Take a look at the code given next; it is very simple and is already contained within our library. It simply checks the logged_in portion of the session data, and if it is TRUE it will return TRUE, allowing the user to proceed to whichever part of the site they're trying to access.

```
<?php

function logged_in()
{

  $CI =& get_instance();

  if($CI->session->userdata('logged_in') == TRUE)
  {
    return TRUE;
  }
  else
  {
    return FALSE;
  }
}

?>
```

CodeIgniter's hidden gems

CodeIgniter is a fairly well equipped framework, and it's easy to let some of its functions slip away from you. This section is dedicated to bringing your attention to some of its lesser-known but also awesome functions, such as:

```
$this->load->helper('html');
```

doctype()

CodeIgniter comes with a function that lets you easily add doctypes to your view files. This is stored in the HTML helper. It will default to XHTML 1.1 Strict, and supports HTML4 and 5 doctypes.

Here's an example of some of the doctypes that you can display by using this function.

```
doctype('html5'); // HTML5
doctype('xhtml11'); // XHTML 1.1
doctype('xhtml1-strict'); // XHTML 1.0 Strict
doctype('xhtml1-trans'); // XHTML 1.0 Transitional
doctype('xhtml1-frame'); // XHTML 1.0 Frameset
doctype('html4-strict'); // HTML 4 Strict
doctype('html4-trans'); // HTML 4 Transitional
doctype('html4-frame'); // HTML 4 Frameset
```

This is very useful because you won't need to find a doctype to copy and paste in from somewhere, or have to remember the doctype yourself. This function also makes it easier to update a doctype on your site quicker than when placing the doctype in there by hand.

Array helper

The array helper has two functions, in it and they are both very useful.

```
$this->load->helper('array');
```

element()

The element function makes it very easy to find an element in an array. If the element doesn't exist, it will return FALSE, or whatever you pass as the third parameter.

```
$items = array(
                'England' => 'London',
                'Wales' => 'Cardiff',
                'Scotland' => 'Edinburgh',
                'Northen Ireland' => 'Belfast');

// returns 'Edinburgh'
echo element('scotland', $items);

// returns FALSE
echo element('france', $items);

// returns NULL
echo element('spain', $items, NULL);
```

random_element()

This function is also very useful. It allows you to pull a random element from an array. Simply echo out the function call with an array passed as the first parameter, and it will return a random element.

```
$items = array(
                'England' => 'London',
                'Wales' => 'Cardiff',
                'Scotland' => 'Edinburgh',
                'Northen Ireland' => 'Belfast');

echo random_element($items);
```

This is useful for random quotes on your website, or a random ad banner.

Inflector helper

The Inflector helper can be a highly useful helper. Its functions allow you to change words into singular, plural, camelcase, underscore-separated, and to humanize sentences that have been separated by underscores. You load the helper as follows:

```
$this->load->helper('inflector');
```

singular()

```
$word = 'computers';
echo singular($word); // returns computer
```

plural()

```
$word = 'computer';
echo plural($word); // returns computers
```

camelize()

```
$word = 'computers_are_awesome';
echo camelize($word); // returns computersAreAwesome

$word = 'computers use electricity';
echo camelize($word); // returns computersUseElectricity
```

underscore()

```
$word = 'computers are overrated';
echo underscore($word); // returns computers_are_overrated
```

humanize()

```
$word = 'computers_are_overrated';
echo humanize($word); // returns Computers Are Overrated
```

highlight_code()

I just found this function. It is a way to highlight a string of code—PHP, HTML, and so on. This function is found in the text helper.

```
$this->load->helper('text');
$code =
  "<html><head><title>Hello, World!</title></head>
    <body><p>Hello, World!</p></body></html>";

echo highlight_code($code);
```

directory_map()

This is a very useful function if you need to do lots of directory traversal. This function reads the directory path and builds an array of all of the directories within the path. All sub-folders will be mapped as well. If you only want to map the top-level directories, then set the second parameter to `TRUE`. Hidden files will not be included in the map by default; to override this, set the third parameter to `TRUE`. Here's an example, taken from the CodeIgniter User Guide.

```
Array
(
   [libraries] => Array
   (
       [0] => benchmark.html
       [1] => config.html
       [database] => Array
       (
             [0] => active_record.html
             [1] => binds.html
             [2] => configuration.html
             [3] => connecting.html
             [4] => examples.html
             [5] => fields.html
```

```
                [6] => index.html
                [7] => queries.html
            )
            [2] => email.html
            [3] => file_uploading.html
            [4] => image_lib.html
            [5] => input.html
            [6] => language.html
            [7] => loader.html
            [8] => pagination.html
            [9] => uri.html
    )
```

This might be especially helpful if you are building an image manager, or something along those lines. This would also be a good debugging tool if you are creating or purging lots of files.

Summary

There we have it. We've extend CodeIgniter to suit our needs, and more. We've seen how we can create extended Controllers to keep functionality in multiple Controllers without repeating ourselves all the time. We've also created our own library, as well as extended a CodeIgniter library. Finally we've gone through CodeIgniter and dug up some real treats—some small functions that work and help in a very big way, especially when used on large projects.

10
Developing and Releasing Code to the Community

Most developers will want to develop code and release it to the community. I would encourage you to release code to the community as it makes the community better and allows you to give something back. This chapter goes into detail about what you could do if you create a library and then want to release into the CodeIgniter community.

In this chapter, you will:

- Learn about the different avenues for finding a library to code
- Learn about the ways in which you can market your library and gain exposure within the community
- Learn the different ways of setting up the database tables for your library
- Learn the importance of writing a user guide for your library
- Learn the best ways to update users
- Learn the best way to introduce new updates
- Learn how to ask for feedback
- Learn how to-and why-you should accept user contributions

Find a need in the community (or fill your own need)

The first thing I did when I wanted to create a library (at first it was just for myself) was fill a need I had. The web app that I was building at the time required quite a comprehensive authentication library. Because CodeIgniter didn't have its own authentication library, I went through these steps and decided to create one myself.

If you don't have a problem that you want to fill, then look on the forums for inspiration. There are numerous forum threads with people discussing ideas for CodeIgniter—ideas that you could use to put into a library. You might see people looking for something and then realize that you also might benefit from that. In this case it would seem very logical to build out that type of library, or even a library extension.

Search for existing solutions

The next thing I did was to look for existing solutions. No matter how much you want to build a library, if there's something out there that does exactly what you want to do and does it well, then there's no point in reinventing the wheel. Here's what to do when you've found a number of solutions. Depending on what type of library you want to build, try to find at least two to three solutions.

Use the solutions

If a solution that you find is actually really good, you might never know it. I always used a number of the libraries I found, just to see if they worked and if they might save me a lot of work in creating my own library.

If the solution that you found doesn't work all that well, or lacks some features, then you'll know what to fix, and what to do differently. This will be a great chance to list all of its shortcomings. Like I said previously, if it's great, there's no point in reinventing the wheel.

Reinvent the wheel

Yes, I did just say there was no point in reinventing the wheel. And yes, this heading tells you to reinvent the wheel. It's not a typo.

The point I'm trying to make with this section is that in most cases, the wheel isn't perfect. Of course by 'wheel' I mean the current implementation of a library.

When I needed an authentication library I tried two different libraries and found them to be difficult to get used to. They didn't handle form processing, and lacked some features. I really tried using them; I prototyped my web app twice, both times scrapping it because the authentication library wasn't good enough.

This ultimately led me to creating **The Authentication Library**—which is extremely easy to use. Simply extend the class 'Application' instead of 'Controller' in your controllers. How much easier can it get?

List the problems of these solutions

By making a list of everything that is missing from the solutions that you've tried, or something that doesn't quite work, or if it could have been done better, is a great way for you to really give something different and better to the community.

This is also a very good lead-in to the next point.

Create a plan

I am an advocate of proper planning and preparation. If your library is quite small, you might get away with not creating a plan. But, if like **The Authentication Library**, your library is quite large and made up of more than a few files, then a plan is a really good idea.

List the features

You should create a list of the features that your library is going to have. This is important to do. Without a list of features, you could start developing the library and then keep adding more and more features as they come up. This is called **scope creep** and could kill your library before you even have a chance to release it. Having a list of features that you need before you start developing will help you stay on track, not allowing any more features to be added until you finish the ones that you have written down and release the library.

If you forget a few of the features that you want, leave them out. Release the features you had in the first place. If you add in the ones that you forgot about, you will be tempted to add in more and more. If you forgot it in the first place, it probably isn't all that important.

Prioritize the features

Now that you have a list of the features that you want your library to have, put them into order. Put the most important features at the top, and the ones you'd just *like* to have at the bottom. Then all you have to do is work your way down the list.

Writing the library

Writing the code is made very easy by having a list of features organized into a priority list. By adding the most important features first, and not the easiest, you are ensuring that you get the features that you really need. So if you end up finishing the code before everything is done, you're more likely to have a fairly well featured library than if you had just developed the easiest things to do first.

You should remember when you're writing the code to make it easy to understand for other people and yourself when you come to view it later on in another project. Leave comments in the code explaining what's going on, wherever you feel necessary.

As you are creating the library, it might be a good idea to create little tests. The tests may only be getting and/or setting session data through your library—but try to get something down just to ensure that the function works. You can create more meaningful tests when the library is deemed 'complete', if you feel the need to.

Review your code

This can be a hard task to do for some people, because some people are not all that suited to finding flaws in code. When you've written your code, you tend to think along the lines of what you've written, instead of thinking things like "How can I make this better?", "How is it valuable?", "Does it work as intended?", and so on.

You can make your code review easier by asking a set of simple questions. Some of which I have already stated.

- How can I make this better?
- Is it as fast as it could be?
- Is it readable to others?
- Have I included relevant comments?
- How will it add value to other people's work?
- Does it do what I say it should do?

You can ask yourself as many questions as you like to ensure that you're churning out the best code you can.

Comments

Before we move on, I want to give you a quick note about comments. Comments should be valuable and help you read the code you've put down. Consider the following comments in your code:

```
// while 1 = 1—print "1 = 1" on the screen

while(1 = 1)
{
  echo "1 = 1";
}
```

The previous comment doesn't help anybody read the code. People will be able to see that there is a while loop and see perfectly clearly what the loop does. It's not a very complex loop. Instead, you should place comments in code to tell people *why* you've done something when things get difficult. If there is a really complicated part of your code that nobody could ever read, explain what the code does and why you made it totally unreadable. There's always a perfectly good explanation for code, you just need to express that in your comments.

Fix the problems

It is inevitable that there will be problems with your code. We always miss something, or a feature we built doesn't work perfectly. What we should do when we have things to fix is create another list. We're going over the same processes used to write the code in the first place. Once you have your list, organize it into priority order, with the highest priority at the top. Then, once again, work your way down the list.

Write a user guide

Once your code is ready, you should write a user guide so that anybody who wants to use your library can simply go to your user guide and read about how to use the functions contained within the library.

Some of the features and functions of your library might be self-explanatory. I know that with The Authentication Library most people don't need to know how to use `login()`, `register()` or `logout()`—you just make a call to them. But others, such as the `restrict()` function, need some explaining.

Explain the function

You should explain what each of your functions does. This could be a single sentence that states the purpose of the function, or it could be a whole paragraph. It all depends on the function that you are describing.

Show the user how to use the function

The next thing that you should do is to give the user an example of how to use the function. It's likely that this might only be a couple of lines of code, but it will make the difference in helping the user gauge how to use the library and decide if it will work for them or not.

Let the user know of any shortcomings

Don't hold false pretenses. Ensure that all functions are documented carefully and that a user wouldn't expect your library to do something that it doesn't. The last thing that you want is a user coming back to you because your library doesn't do what they thought it would, or that your user guide says it works in one way, when it actually works slightly differently. Now, I'm not sure somebody in the CodeIgniter community would ever be that banal, its just a matter of being prepared for any problems that might occur.

Use the style sheet given in the CodeIgniter User Guide

The CodeIgniter User Guide is awesome. In fact, I know a number of people who started using CodeIgniter simply because the User Guide is brilliant and tells you everything that you need to know about the framework, and is always kept up to date.

The guys at EllisLab know this, and provide a stylesheet and example page so that you can create user guides for your own libraries that look just like the official CodeIgniter User Guide. You can access these yourself, by visiting their site at `http://codeigniter.com/user_guide/doc_style/index.html`, as seen in the next screenshot.

I believe this is beneficial to developers, as developers are comfortable with the CodeIgniter User Guide style and if you carry that on with your own user guide then you can only make them feel more comfortable by doing so.

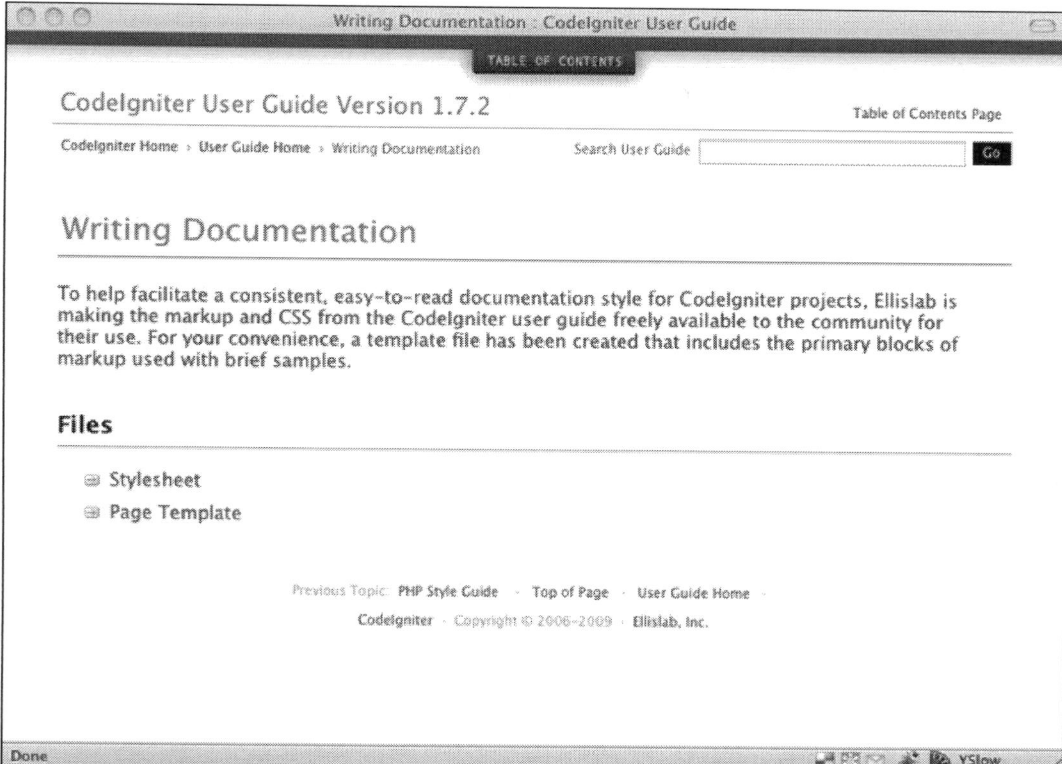

Release options

When you come to release your library there are a number of things I would suggest that you do in order to get more exposure and make it easier for developers to download and use your library.

Forum post

A forum post is the least that you should do to tell people about your library. Simply create a new post in the '**Ignited Code**' section at `http://codeigniter.com/forums/` and tell people about your library. Be sure to put the features that it has in the post so that people know what to expect. You don't have to put every little detail into it; just indicate some of the more important features.

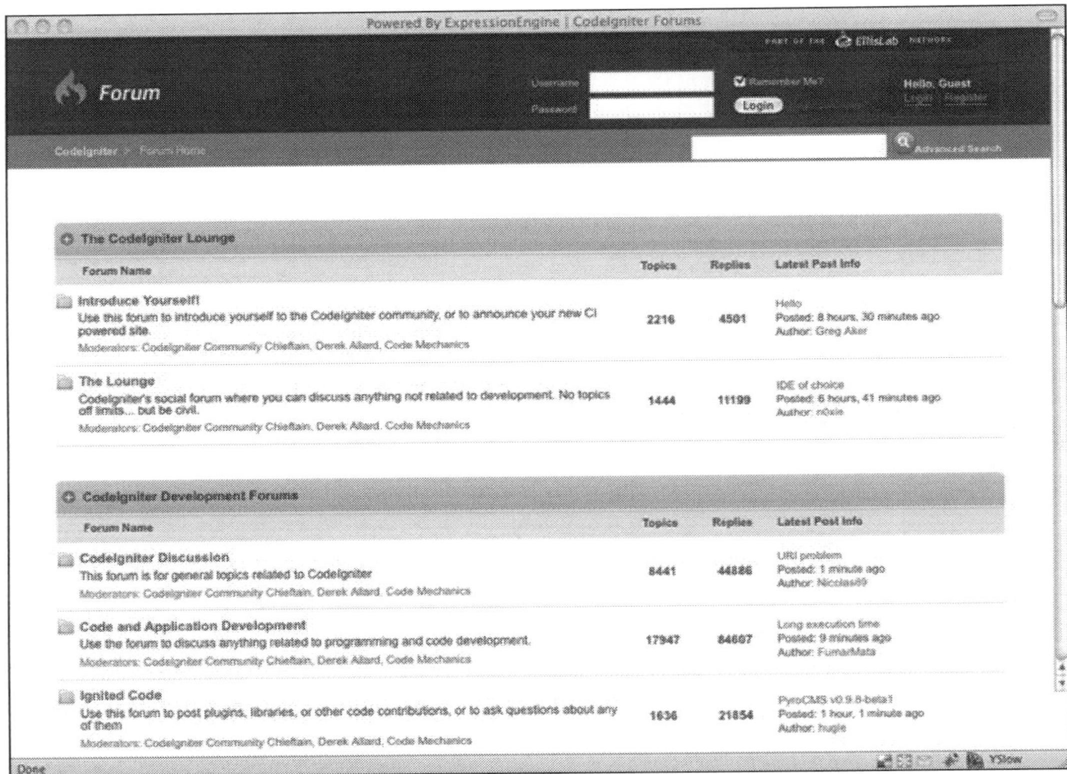

Post on your website

If you have a website of blog I also suggest making a post on there to direct people to your Library User Guide or a GitHub repository. Obviously, only post on your website or blog if it is related to CodeIgniter—don't post about your new library if you run a photography blog, for example. The tips for a forum post apply here, as well. In fact you could post the same thing on both the forum post and your website.

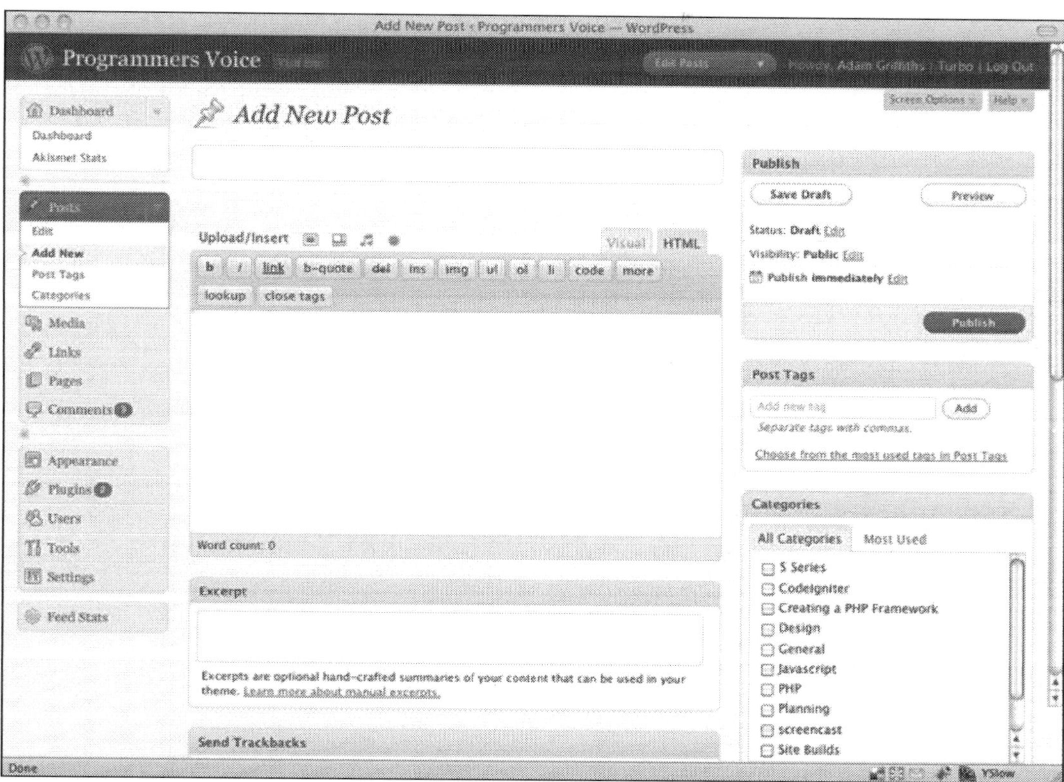

GitHub

GitHub is a social network built around sharing code. It is comprised of Git repositories that developers set up to allow other developers to easily download their code, or fork it to create a new project. You can follow other developers to keep up to date with what they're doing, and also watch specific repositories, at `http://github.com`.

GitHub is a great way to maintain a library because it also comes with issue tracking. So if somebody finds a problem with the library, they can create a new ticket in the issue tracker instead of emailing you directly. This keeps everything related to your library on the GitHub repository site, and helps you to better organize things.

The best thing about it, though, is that it is based on Git repositories. Git is a revision control system that helps you manage version of your software, and helps you to roll back changes if you need to.

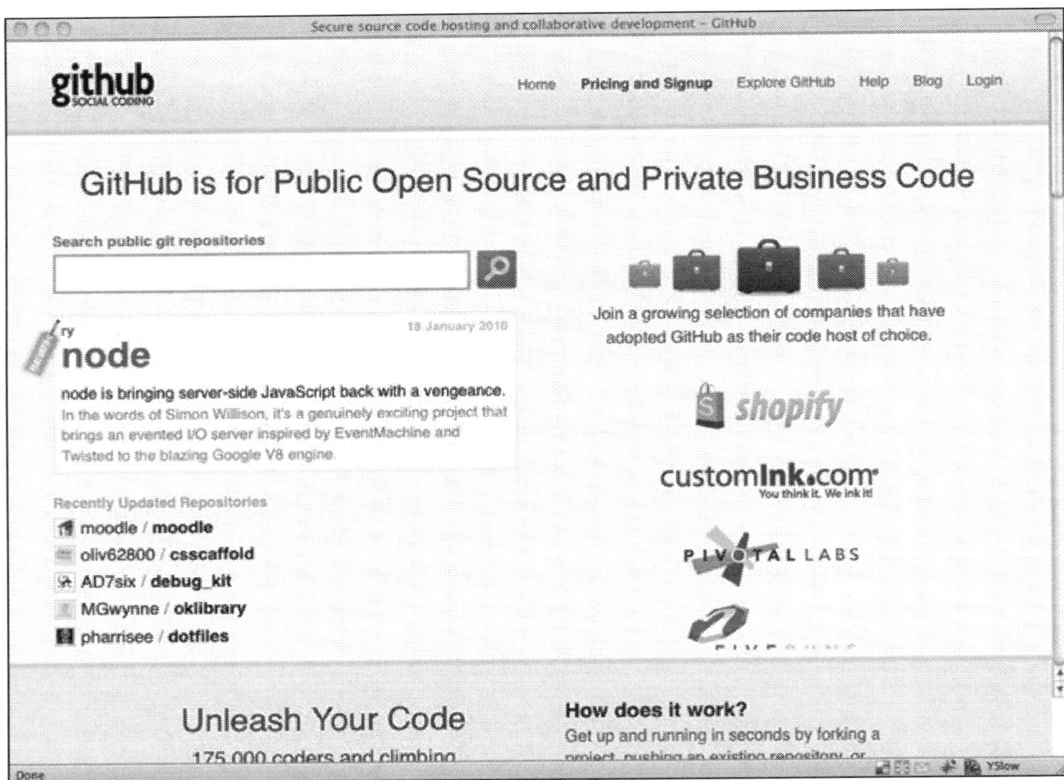

Handling database tables

You might find that your library needs to make use of a database table. There are a few ways that you can go about including a database table, but which way is the best?

Include a .sql file

Personally, this is my preferred method of including a database table with my libraries.

I simply include a `.sql` file, along with all of the MySQL queries needed to create all of the tables. This is the easiest method of including a way to create the tables for the library developer, although it's not so easy for the developer trying to use the library. It's not ideal, but it works well.

Include an install file

Another method would be to create an install file that connects to the database and creates all of the tables. The problem with this method is that it takes time to build and you don't know how far to go with it. Do you ask for the database details? Do you write over `config/database.php`?

To be honest with you, I feel that an install file for a library would be total overkill. You could end up writing more code for the installer than the library itself. The previous method is quicker, and most developers see a `.sql` file and immediately know what to do with it.

Supporting the code

Now that you've got your code out there and people are using it, you'll probably want to start supporting your code. Here are some easy steps to follow to make sure that you keep the developers who are using your code in the loop, and to help you update your code with valuable additions.

Update regularly

Once your library is out there, you will ultimately come up with new ideas for features that you want to include. The original version of my authentication library was fairly simple and lacked some features. The next version I created included groups and a more comprehensive restrict function. Then I went further and made it so that the developer could call their database tables anything, and made it generally easier to fit into an existing project. Finally I made it so that the only thing a developer needs to do to use the library is extend a different Controller class (Application). This includes form validation and all the backend functions too.

See how the code developed over time? I didn't think of everything and include it all right from the start. The code would be too complex to do that right from the beginning. The same will happen with your code. Ultimately you'll create what you think you need; once you start using it you might want to add more and more. This is great.

Try not to update the code too regularly, though. I remember when releasing version 1.0.1 of The Authentication Library I had missed out some of the features that people had recommended, and as a result I released 1.0.2 a day after 1.0.1. This means that developers had to upgrade twice in two days. Make sure you don't do this; try to bunch up the additions so that when you release an updated version there is enough in there to justify the user upgrading.

Listen to the users

The more people that use your code, the better the code you will write. This essentially means that you have many more reviewers of your code. Users can post in the CodeIgniter forum thread that you created and talk to you directly about the code, how it works, and so on. They can also talk to other people using your library as well.

Mostly, though, people will make recommendations and request other features. I wouldn't suggest adding in everything that a user asks for; sometimes it is better to leave a feature out. I always say to myself "*If this addition is only going to benefit the user requesting it, then I'm not going to build it for them*". That statement might make me look like I don't care, but I want my additions to benefit as many people as possible; and if I make an addition and people question me as to why I added something in, I don't want to reply "*Oh because Mr X asked me for it.*"

I recommend that other developers really evaluate how an extra feature will benefit you and the other developers using it.

Accept contributions

I always find it extremely helpful when a user asks me for an extra feature, and somebody else replies with an updated version of my library with it already added in. In most cases the user will be glad to have their contribution included in the library, and I am always glad to put other people's code in my Library. In fact, it's an open source library, so no one person really 'owns' it.

Of course, proper testing will need to be performed for the code. Try to devise a short checklist for code that you get from others. If it ticks all of the boxes, then you could add it to the main code.

Communicate regularly

You should keep the community updated as to what you're doing with the code. You could update your forum thread with the features that you'll be adding into the library. This not only helps people to know what to expect, but also cements the features. It also ensures that you build those features. If you say that you'll build something publically and you don't, then people will question you. This is good because it makes you more reliable; nobody wants to be questioned. That's why, when you announce you'll build something on the forums, you will build it and it will be added into your library.

EllisLab, the company behind CodeIgniter and the popular web publishing platform ExpressionEngine, did this when they were developing ExpressionEngine 2.0. EllisLab gave regular updates to the developers on their blog, giving screenshots and explaining new features and even how they went about creating some of the new features.

Take a leaf out of EllisLab's book if you need to; it worked perfectly, kept developers in the loop, and kept everyone excited about the new software.

Don't give a release date

From past experience, I can tell you that it is a very bad idea to give a release date for code before it's ready. If your code is done, its fine to say "*I will release this code on Monday*". However, never declare a release date before the code is ready.

EllisLab found this out when developing ExpressionEngine 2.0. Their original release date was blown out of the water and the software was released a year later. But they worked through it by updating regularly.

We all know the importance of releasing only when the code is ready, and when we're not ready to release, keep the developers who depend on us in the loop.

As soon as the code is ready, however, you have two options. You can give a release date and create some hype behind the new version, or you could simply release the code on GitHub and post on the forums again. It is totally up to you and it really depends on how you like to work. Personally, I just get the code out there and tweet about it, blog about it, and post in the forums.

Keep testing

Just because your original code worked doesn't mean that new additions will. Before releasing any new versions of the library make sure you test all the new code *and test* the old features too. I have released new code a few times and found out the old stuff was affected by it.

I cannot stress how important proper code testing is. The last thing that you want is for people on the forums to be telling you that something's broken. Find out all the kinks before you release, and remove them.

Archive old versions

I found it is a very good idea to archive the old versions of your code. This is especially easy if you use a Version Control System such as Git or SVN. This is helpful for developers when you release a new update as your new code could interfere with their code and it helps them roll back the version easily. Of course, they should be testing as well, but it is always nice to have another failsafe, in any event.

Use the wiki

This is a good idea and one that isn't used by quite a few developers I know. The wiki is a great place to look for code and sometimes people always overlook it. Create a short wiki entry for your library at `http://codeigniter.com/wiki/`. It won't take that long and you could even use the copy from your forum post. It is simply another possible point of exposure for your library and will ultimately help people to find you and your library.

The wiki is a perfect format for easily keeping your users informed as well. If there is a small code fix that wouldn't warrant a new update and is fairly small, you can put it in the forum thread. This, however, will be harder to find, when compared to searching on the wiki page.

You should make sure that as many people as possible know about the wiki entry. It can be very helpful to use but it is all useless if people don't actually know about the entry. Whenever you post a link to GitHub (or wherever you hold your user guide or other download point) include a link to the wiki entry.

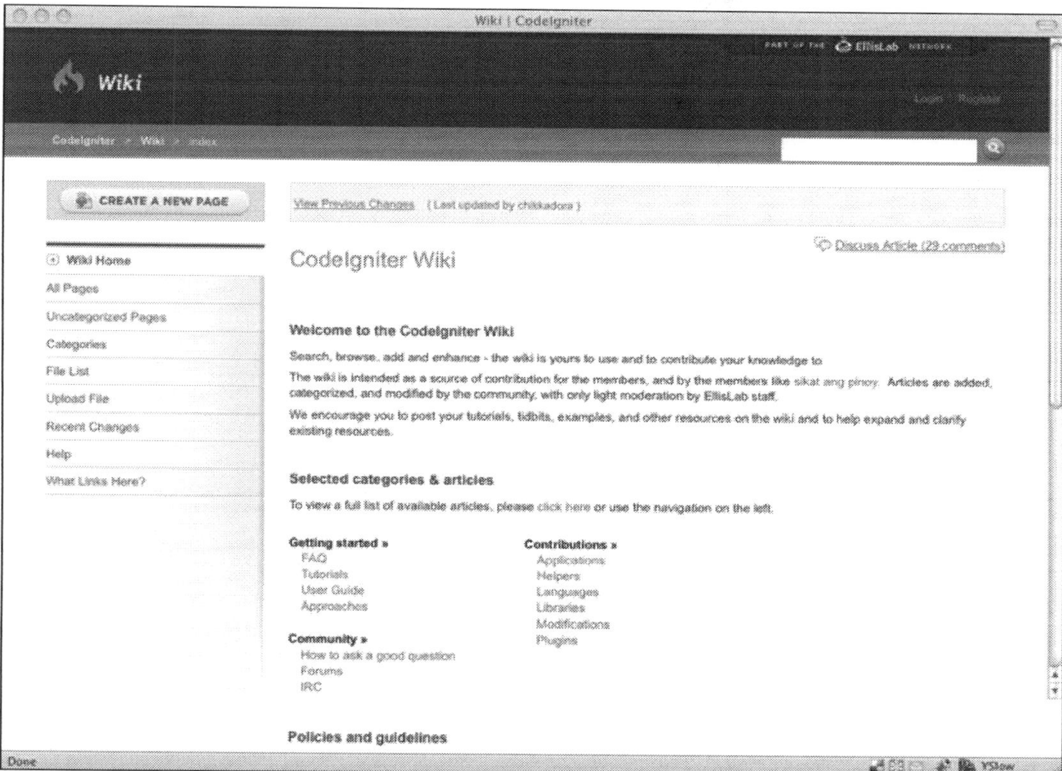

Summary

The steps in this chapter are all fairly easy to do and don't take too much time. But when you put them all together they serve as a great platform to develop code with and support both the code and end users. This chapter should also help you to streamline the process and better manage the code that you release.

Index

Symbols

A

B

C

D

E

F

G

H

Q

R

S

T

Thank you for buying

CodeIgniter 1.7 Professional Development

About Packt Publishing

Packt, pronounced 'packed', published its first book "*Mastering phpMyAdmin for Effective MySQL Management*" in April 2004 and subsequently continued to specialize in publishing highly focused books on specific technologies and solutions.

Our books and publications share the experiences of your fellow IT professionals in adapting and customizing today's systems, applications, and frameworks. Our solution based books give you the knowledge and power to customize the software and technologies you're using to get the job done. Packt books are more specific and less general than the IT books you have seen in the past. Our unique business model allows us to bring you more focused information, giving you more of what you need to know, and less of what you don't.

Packt is a modern, yet unique publishing company, which focuses on producing quality, cutting-edge books for communities of developers, administrators, and newbies alike. For more information, please visit our website: `www.packtpub.com`.

About Packt Open Source

In 2010, Packt launched two new brands, Packt Open Source and Packt Enterprise, in order to continue its focus on specialization. This book is part of the Packt Open Source brand, home to books published on software built around Open Source licences, and offering information to anybody from advanced developers to budding web designers. The Open Source brand also runs Packt's Open Source Royalty Scheme, by which Packt gives a royalty to each Open Source project about whose software a book is sold.

Writing for Packt

We welcome all inquiries from people who are interested in authoring. Book proposals should be sent to author@packtpub.com. If your book idea is still at an early stage and you would like to discuss it first before writing a formal book proposal, contact us; one of our commissioning editors will get in touch with you.

We're not just looking for published authors; if you have strong technical skills but no writing experience, our experienced editors can help you develop a writing career, or simply get some additional reward for your expertise.

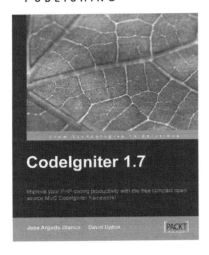

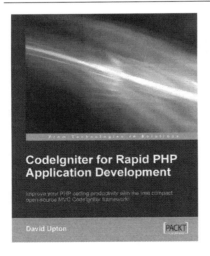

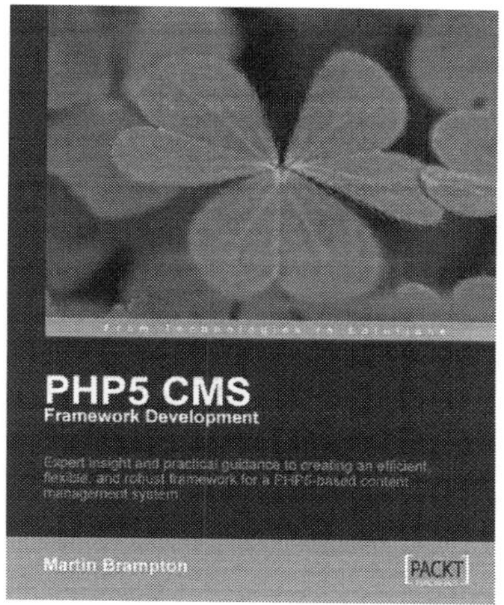

PHP 5 CMS Framework Development

ISBN: 978-1-847193-57-5 Paperback: 348 pages

Expert insight and practical guidance to creating an efficient, flexible, and robust framework for a PHP 5-based content management system

1. Learn how to design, build, and implement a complete CMS framework for your custom requirements
2. Implement a solid architecture with object orientation, MVC
3. Build an infrastructure for custom menus, modules, components, sessions, user tracking, and more
4. Written by a seasoned developer of CMS applications

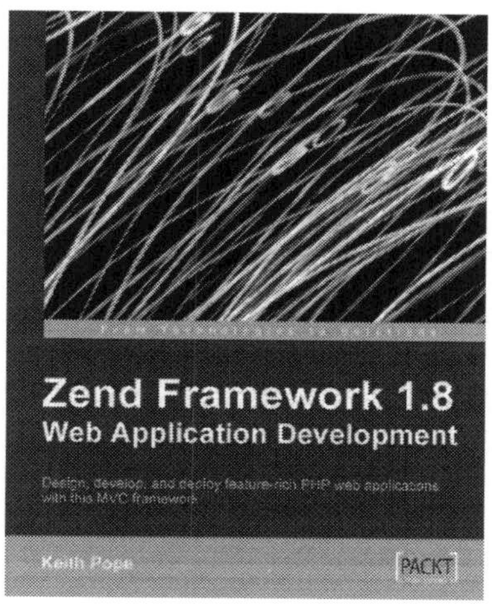

Zend Framework 1.8 Web Application Development

ISBN: 978-1-847194-22-0 Paperback: 380 pages

Design, develop, and deploy feature-rich PHP web applications with this MVC framework

1. Create powerful web applications by leveraging the power of this Model-View-Controller-based framework
2. Learn by doing – create a "real-life" storefront application
3. Covers access control, performance optimization, and testing
4. Best practices, as well as debugging and designing discussion

Please check **www.PacktPub.com** for information on our titles

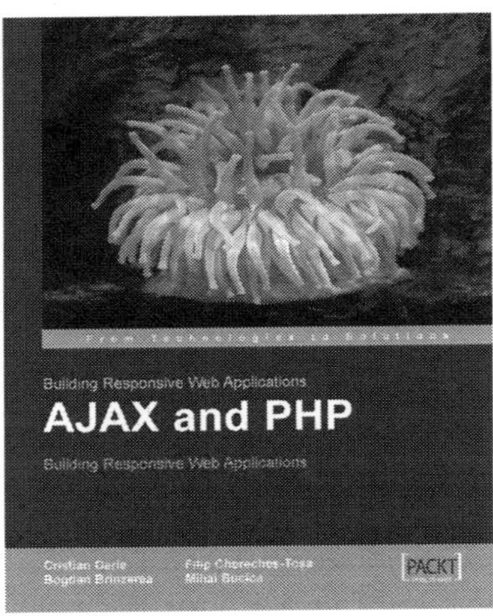

AJAX and PHP: Building Responsive Web Applications

ISBN: 1-90-4811-82-5 Paperback: 284 pages

Enhance the user experience of your PHP website using AJAX with this practical tutorial featuring detailed case studies

1. Build a solid foundation for your next generation of web applications
2. Use better JavaScript code to enable powerful web features
3. Leverage the power of PHP and MySQL to create powerful back-end functionality and make it work in harmony with the smart AJAX client

---

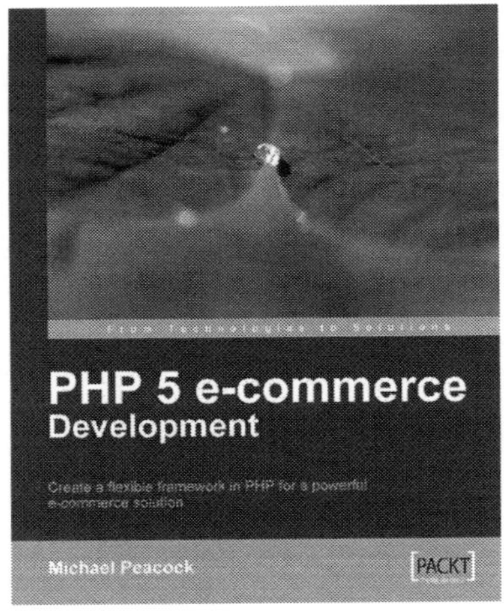

PHP 5 E-commerce Development

ISBN: 978-1-847199-64-5 Paperback: 356 pages

Create a flexible framework in PHP for a powerful ecommerce solution

1. Build a flexible e-commerce framework using PHP, which can be extended and modified for the purposes of any e-commerce site
2. Enable customer retention and more business by creating rich user experiences
3. Develop a suitable structure for your framework and create a registry to store core objects
4. Promote your e-commerce site using techniques with APIs such as Google Products or Amazon web services, SEO, marketing, and customer satisfaction

Please check **www.PacktPub.com** for information on our titles

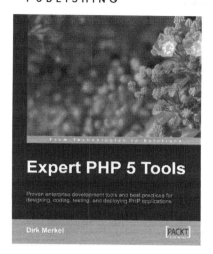

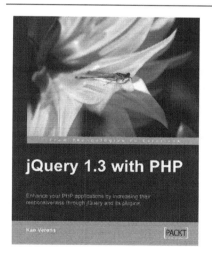

15540024R00160

Made in the USA
Lexington, KY
02 June 2012